RACIAL DISCRIMINATION:
Your Right to Equal Opportunity

Acknowledgments

I am most grateful to Raymond Halliwell, Bolton's Community Relations Officer, for his most useful comments on a number of points. I should, however, make it clear that all the opinions expressed in this book are my own and that I accept full responsibility for the contents of the book.

My thanks also to Shirley Cannon for typing the successive drafts of the book.

I dedicate this book to Kate and my parents.

RACIAL DISCRIMINATION:
Your Right to Equal Opportunity

Michael Malone

Ross Anderson Publications

First published in 1983 by
ROSS ANDERSON PUBLICATIONS
22 Higher Dunscar
Egerton, Bolton BL7 9TE

**British Library Cataloguing in
Publication Data**

Malone, Michael
   Racial discrimination
   1. Race discrimination – Law and
      legislation –
      Great Britain
   I. Title
   344.102'873   KD4095

ISBN 0–86360–004–2

Photoset in Plantin by
Northern Phototypesetting Co., Bolton
Printed in England by
Billings of Worcester

Foreword

If you have a black or brown skin you are unlikely to go through life in Great Britain without meeting some racial discrimination. The discrimination is most likely to occur and is most serious in its consequences for you when you are applying for a job or promotion or when you are looking for a house to rent. You could also face discrimination at work, when you are trying to enter a place of entertainment, when you want to buy goods on credit, in connection with your education or your child's education or even when you are trying to start your own business.

A white skin does not always protect you from racial discrimination, especially if you are of foreign nationality or descent.

Even if you never experience discrimination personally, advising victims of discrimination may be part of your job or your voluntary work, for example if you are a shop steward or a helper at an advice centre or a worker in community relations.

This book explains your rights and the rights of those you may have to advise. It does so in ordinary language and most points are illustrated with examples, some based on real cases.

The book answers several questions. What is racial discrimination? When is discrimination unlawful? Are there any exceptions? What rights do you have if someone discriminates against you? How can you go about claiming those rights? The book does not only say what racial discrimination is but also contains practical advice on how to recognise racial discrimination and do something about it.

Whatever kind of discrimination you are interested in, you should read the Introduction to this book before turning to the appropriate part of the book. The Introduction explains some of the general principles which are relevant to any claim of discrimination.

The book takes into account changes in the law up to 31st March, 1983.

Readers in Scotland should bear in mind that Scotland has sheriff courts instead of county courts and a different education system from England and Wales.

Contents

Part I – Looking for Work

Part II – Discrimination at Work

Part III – Discrimination to do with Houses and Flats

Part IV – Other Acts of Discrimination

Part V – The Self-Employed

Introduction

The main purpose of this Introduction is to explain what racial discrimination is, in what circumstances you have your right to equal opportunity and what you can do about it if someone does discriminate against you. Then there are one or two notes about this book and finally some of the reasons why we need a Race Relations Act are explained.

What is racial discrimination?

The Race Relations Act covers three kinds of discrimination. There is direct discrimination, there is indirect discrimination and there is victimisation. We shall see that it is quite easy to understand what is meant by direct discrimination and victimisation, but it can be quite difficult to spot these kinds of discrimination when they actually happen. The meaning of indirect discrimination is rather more complicated.

There is another important difference between indirect discrimination and the other kinds of discrimination. If you take your case to a court or an industrial tribunal and prove direct discrimination against you or victimisation, the court or tribunal always has the power to make an order for compensation to be paid to you. Sometimes (but not always) when it is indirect discrimination that you are complaining about you can win your case but still not be entitled to compensation.

Direct discrimination

Direct discrimination happens when on racial grounds you are treated less favourably than somebody else is treated or would be treated. If, for example, you are turned down for a job and somebody of a different colour is appointed, this would be direct racial discrimination if the decision to turn you down was made on racial grounds.

What does "on racial grounds" mean? It does not refer only to your colour. It also covers your nationality, your race and your ethnic or national origins. There is direct racial discrimination against you if you are treated unfavourably because you are white, brown, black or yellow; because you are English, Welsh, Scots or Irish; because you have foreign nationality; because you or your parents or some more distant ancestor came from India, Bangladesh, the West Indies or any other country; or because you are Jewish.

This definition of direct discrimination is a very wide one. It even covers the following example:

i   You are white. You apply for a job but are turned down because your wife is black. The refusal of your application for the job is direct racial discrimination against you.

When you are trying to recognise whether direct discrimination has occurred, the important question is what the person treating you unfavourably believed about you. For example:

ii   You make a written application for a job. The employer to whom you apply is prejudiced against the Irish and he turns you down because your name is Michael Malone. This is direct racial discrimination, even though the employer is wrong in his belief and you are not Irish.

The Court of Appeal has recently ruled* that there can still be racial discrimination even though your colour or some other racial factor was not the only reason you were treated unfavourably. As long as your colour or the other racial factor plays an important part in the decision made there is direct racial discrimination. For example:

iii   You are black and you and a white person apply for the same job. You are more highly qualified but the white person has more

---

* Owen & Briggs v. James [1982] Industrial Relations Law Reports, 502.

experience. The employer decides that the other applicant's colour and greater experience, taken together, outweigh your better qualifications and gives the other applicant the job. The employer has discriminated against you even though your colour was not the only reason for turning you down.

Indirect discrimination

In order to prove indirect discrimination against you, you have to show that four questions should be answered yes. Has some requirement or condition been applied to you? Have you been unable to comply with it? Has this inability been to your disadvantage? Is the proportion of the members of your racial group who cannot comply with the requirement considerably greater than the proportion of other people who cannot comply with it?

These questions sound complicated, especially the last one. In practice, however, courts and tribunals hearing discrimination cases adopt a sensible attitude and usually do not insist on having pages of statistics to prove obvious points. You will often have little difficulty in showing that a requirement is discriminatory in its effect, especially when what is required is ability to speak or write English or some educational qualification. For example:

iv   You are of Pakistani origin. You apply for a job as a labourer. You can understand English well but you can speak hardly any. The employer refuses to consider you for the job because you cannot speak English. If you take your case to an industrial tribunal you will have little difficulty in showing that the four questions should be answered yes. The employer has applied to you the requirement that you must be able to speak English. You cannot comply with this requirement. This inability has been to your disadvantage, because it has denied you the opportunity of being considered for the job. So far as the fourth question is concerned, you must give evidence that the proportion of Pakistanis in Great Britain who cannot speak English is considerably greater than the corresponding proportion of non-Pakistanis (who include the millions of white people in Great Britain who have been brought up to speak English). The members of the tribunal will be sensible and practical people and they are likely readily to accept your evidence without requiring detailed statistics showing the exact proportion of Pakistanis or Pakistani labourers in Great Britain who cannot speak English and the corresponding proportion of non-Pakistanis.

Even if you can show that the requirement or condition is indirectly discriminatory in its effect on you and members of your racial group, your claim can still be defeated, if the requirement or condition can be shown to be justifiable. In the above example the employer would have great difficulty in showing this, because being able to speak English well does not make you a better labourer. However, sometimes it is more difficult to predict whether a court or tribunal will find a requirement or condition to be justifiable. This question will be considered in more detail in Chapter 4, in the context of applications for jobs.

Even if the discriminatory requirement or condition is not shown to be justifiable and you win your case, this is not the end of the story. The main remedy which courts and tribunals have the power to give you is to make an order for the person whom you are complaining about to pay compensation to you. However, when you are complaining about indirect discrimination, the court or tribunal has no power to order the payment of compensation if it is shown that the requirement or condition is not racially motivated. In the above example, the employer would not be ordered to pay you compensation if he satisfied the tribunal members that the requirement that you should be able to speak English was not something which he had dreamed up so as to give him an excuse for not taking on you and other coloured applicants for jobs. The tribunal members would not easily be convinced of this, but they could be if, for example, they heard and believed evidence from the employer to the effect that he was genuinely concerned to take on workers who could easily communicate with each other and thereby create a happy atmosphere at work and that he had employed a number of Asian workers who could speak English.

On the other hand, the law does not permit a person to get away with discrimination by making up an artificial requirement or condition. For example:

v   You came to England twenty years ago from India. You apply for the tenancy of a house. The landlord asks you how long you have lived in England and tells you that he is not prepared to consider letting his house to anyone who has not lived in England for at least twenty five years. The requirement, that in order to be considered for the tenancy you must have lived in England for at least twenty five years, is discriminatory against you as a person of Indian origin. Furthermore the requirement is clearly one which has been made up in order to make it more likely that the landlord will be able to obtain a white tenant without openly discriminating on racial grounds. If you take your case to the county court the landlord will not be able to prove that the requirement was not racially motivated and accordingly you will be entitled to damages.

Requirements not applied equally

Furthermore, if a requirement or condition is not applied equally to people of different racial groups then this is direct discrimination, not indirect. For example:

vi   You are of West Indian origin. You apply for a job. You are required to take an intelligence test. White applicants are not required to take the test. The employer is discriminating against you directly by requiring you, and not other applicants, to take an intelligence test and doing so because of your colour or national origin.

Meaning of "requirement or condition"

There is a further important point. The Court of Appeal has ruled* that there is a difference between a requirement or condition, which can operate as an absolute bar to (say) a job or promotion, and a factor which is taken into account but which does not operate as an absolute bar. This was a case where a highly qualified civil servant from Sri Lanka applied for a more senior post. He was a member of the English

* Perera v. Civil Service Commission, *The Times*, 7th February 1983.

5

Bar and accordingly satisfied the only formal requirement for the job. The board which interviewed him also took into account, amongst other factors, the extent of his experience in the United Kingdom and his command of the English language. He complained that there had been indirect discrimination. However, the court ruled that if an employer does not absolutely rule out applicants who do not have sufficient command of English or sufficient experience in the United Kingdom, but simply takes these factors into account when making a selection, there is no question of indirect discrimination.

Sikhs and Jews

A recent decision* of the House of Lords has clarified the law in two important respects.

First, the expression "racial group" must be defined widely. In words which were adopted by Lord Fraser, people can belong to the same racial group if "they have a distinct social identity based not simply on group cohesion and solidarity but also on their belief as to their historical antecedents." The Sikhs are a racial group; so are the Jews; so probably are the Romany people.

Indirect discrimination against Sikhs is most likely to arise when they face a requirement as to their dress or appearance. In the above House of Lords case, a Sikh schoolboy had been refused a place at a private school because he was not prepared to comply with a school rule that he should wear uniform and not a turban. In one sense, the school's requirement was one with which he could have complied. It was not physically impossible for him to leave his turban at home. However the House of Lords held that he could not comply with the requirement. The expression "cannot comply" is not to be interpreted literally. It means "cannot in practice comply" or "cannot comply consistently with the customs and cultural conditions of your racial group".

In the above case the House of Lords also held that the requirement

* Mandla and Mandla v. Lee and Park Grove Private School Limited. *The Times*, 25th March, 1983.

was not justifiable and accordingly the schoolboy and his father succeeded in their claim.

Victimisation

The consequences of victimisation are the same as those of direct racial discrimination. You are victimised if you are treated unfavourably because you have made an allegation of racial discrimination or brought proceedings or given evidence in proceedings or taken any other action under the Race Relations Act. For example:

vii   You are white. A black colleague who has been refused a promotion brings a complaint of discrimination and you give evidence on behalf of your colleague, whose claim is successful. The following year, when wages are reviewed, everybody else is given an increase but your wage remains the same. If you can show that you have been refused a wage increase because you gave evidence on behalf of your colleague then you will succeed in a claim against your employer under the Race Relations Act.

There is one important qualification. If you make an allegation against your employer and that allegation is false and not made in good faith, then you cannot complain under the Race Relations Act if the employer penalises you for the allegation. For example:

viii   You complain about racial harassment at work and take your case to a tribunal. Your complaint is dismissed. In their written decision the tribunal state that they did not believe your evidence and they believe that you brought the case only because you have a personal grudge against your superior at work. As a result, the employer refuses to consider you for promotion for which you would otherwise have been eligible. This refusal is not regarded as discrimination for the purposes of the Race Relations Act.

In what circumstances does the law forbid discrimination against you?

In considering what is meant by racial discrimination, we have touched on some examples of the circumstances in which discrimination is forbidden. Many others are given in Part I which deals with your right to equal opportunity when you are looking for work. This is the longest Part of the book partly because your right to equal opportunity when looking for work is one of your most important rights, partly because many of the complaints of racial discrimination have been about discrimination against applicants for jobs and partly because discrimination in these circumstances can be very difficult to prove. This Part of the book explains what your rights are and points out that you have rights not only against employers but also against other individuals or bodies involved with employment or training, such as trade unions, employment agencies and training bodies. There is then a chapter which shows how you may be able to recognise direct discrimination against you and later on prove that it has happened and another chapter giving some examples of the most common kinds of indirect discrimination. The last chapter in this Part explains the steps which you can take if someone has unlawfully discriminated against you.

Once you have been successful in obtaining a job, you have a right to equal opportunity at work. Part II deals with your rights against your employer, with special emphasis on your rights in respect of promotion and training.

One of your most important rights outside the employment field is your right to equal opportunity when you are looking for a house or flat to buy or rent. Part III explains your rights against people who are selling or renting their houses, estate agents, private and local authority landlords, accommodation bureaux and building societies, insurance companies, local authorities and others who provide finance for the purchase of houses. At the beginning of this Part there is a chapter which explains the steps which you can take if someone discriminates against you unlawfully outside the employment field.

This first chapter of Part III is also relevant to the rights explained in Part IV. This Part is mainly about the right to equal opportunity which you enjoy as a member of the public. It includes your rights as a consumer, your rights when you want to use public entertainment or recreation facilities or join a private club and your rights in respect of your education or your child's education.

Part V is the shortest Part of the book. If you are a self-employed business man, you are more likely to have a claim brought against you, by your employees or your customers, rather than be bringing a claim against someone else. For example, if you are a shopkeeper you cannot refuse, on racial grounds, to serve a customer but there is nothing you can do about it if customers boycott your shop because of the colour of your skin. However, there are some circumstances in which the self-employed have a right to equal opportunity and these are explained in the last chapter of the book.

Territorial Extent

The law applies to acts of discrimination which occur in England, Wales and Scotland (and on most British ships and aircraft). You can do nothing about discrimination against you as a job applicant or employee if the work involved is wholly or mainly outside Great Britain (and not on a British ship or aircraft).

When is discrimination permitted?

There is no general rule that racial discrimination against you is always unlawful in whatever circumstances. You only have a right to equal opportunity in the circumstances which have been outlined above and which are considered in more detail in each Part of the book. You cannot go to the courts to complain of racial discrimination against you in someone's private, social or domestic arrangements. If your neighbour, because you are coloured, refuses to invite you in for a drink or speak to you over the garden fence or give you a lift to work there is nothing at all that you can do about it.

Even the rights which you do have are subject to some exceptions, although these are mostly very limited. For example, we shall see in Chapter 2 in Part I that employers are occasionally permitted to discriminate on racial grounds in deciding whom to employ. There are also some general exceptions which can apply in any circumstances. One of these exceptions is not of much practical importance. Whenever any charitable benefits are being handed out then as long as there is no direct discrimination against you on the ground of your colour there can be direct discrimination on other ground discrimination so long as this discrimination is necessi comply with the terms of the charitable trust. Examples of this exception will be considered in Chapter 2 and Chapter 16.

There are two more important general exceptions to your rights. First, racial discrimination against you is always lawful if it is authorised by an Act of Parliament or a statutory regulation or the Immigration Rules. Apart from this exception, you have the same rights against government departments and other public bodies as against anybody else.

Secondly, there is a general exception under which local authorities, employers and others can sometimes discriminate against you when offering education, training or welfare facilities to somebody else and not to you. The discrimination can be lawful if it is to meet the special needs of an ethnic minority, such as a special need for language tuition. Examples of this kind of permitted discrimination will be seen in Chapters 2 and 16.

Apart from this exception, and one or two more limited exceptions, which will be considered in Chapters 2 and 6, the law makes no distinction between positive discrimination and any other kind of racial discrimination. You do not need to be a member of an ethnic minority in order to have rights under the Race Relations Act. For example:

ix   You are white and you apply for a job as a shop assistant. The owner of the shop is Indian and he refuses to consider you for the job. He wants to help a fellow Indian who is less fortunate than himself and he intends to keep the job open until an Indian applies for the job. This discrimination against you is unlawful.

Discrimination must be against you personally

The law gives you rights only when you personally have been the victim of discrimination in circumstances where the law makes that discrimination unlawful. The law gives you no right of action where you are upset by seeing discrimination against somebody else. You also have no personal right to complain about any racialist remarks which are not tied up with the treatment of you as an individual.

For example, if a political organisation pushes through your letterbox a pamphlet which is insulting and inflammatory, there is no court action which you can take personally. All you can do is report the matter to the police so that the Attorney General can be asked to consider authorising a prosecution for incitement to racial hatred.

If you are upset by a discriminatory advertisement for a job not because you wish to apply for the job but because you find the advertisement insulting to members of your racial group, you cannot personally take any proceedings against the advertiser. Only the Commission for Racial Equality has the power to take proceedings in respect of a breach of the law against discriminatory advertisements. If you report the facts to the Commission they will then consider whether to take any action.

Finally, if you read a book or see a play or a film which was written when racial attitudes were different from those of today neither you nor the Commission for Racial Equality has any right of action if you are upset by the role in which members of your ethnic group are portrayed or the remarks made about them.

What can you do about discrimination?

The one thing which the law cannot do for you is give you a non-financial benefit which has been denied to you. If, for example, you have been turned down for a job, then presumably it is a job that you still want, not just compensation. The tribunal cannot make the employer offer you a job. If you are successful in your claim you will usually be awarded compensation (except sometimes when you are complaining about indirect discrimination). The amount awarded to you can include something to compensate you for any injury to your feelings. In theory, the total compensation can amount to several thousand pounds, but it is rare for an award of compensation to approach even one thousand pounds. The most that the tribunal can do to persuade the employer to offer you a job is to make a recommendation to that effect and to allow you to come back for more compensation if the employer unreasonably fails to comply with the recommendation.

Claims of discrimination against employers and other cases in the employment field, which are dealt with in Parts I and II of this book, are heard by industrial tribunals. Complaints outside the employment field are heard by county court judges. The industrial tribunals have been established to deal generally with most claims to do with employment, including unfair dismissal cases against employers. Cases are heard, usually in public, by a tribunal of three members, including a legally qualified chairman. The other two members will have been chosen for their knowledge or experience of industry, one on the management side and the other on the trade union side. Their procedure is less formal than court procedure and the tribunal members are meant to bring to the cases that they hear their practical knowledge of how industry actually works.

The various steps which you should take when your complaint is to do with employment are set out in Chapter 5 in Part I. Chapter 9 indicates, in much less detail, some of the rules which apply when your claim is outside the employment field and you have to take your case to a county court. However, there are one or two general points which should be mentioned here.

Time limits

There is a very short time limit for starting proceedings. In cases which have to go to an industrial tribunal the time limit is only three months. In other cases the time limit is six months (but subject to an extension of two months when you have applied to the Commission for Racial Equality for assistance).

It is vital that, if you wish to take your case to a court or tribunal, you should comply with the time limit. The court or tribunal has the power to extend the time limit, but will consider doing so only where there has been a very good reason for the delay.

Help with your case

In most successful claims of discrimination the complainant has had the benefit of being represented at the court or tribunal hearing, either by a solicitor or by another expert, such as a complaints officer from the Commission for Racial Equality. There is an important difference here between industrial tribunal cases and county court cases. You can apply for legal aid to take proceedings in the county court. If your income and capital are low enough and you can show reasonable grounds for starting the proceedings then you will be able to have a solicitor to prepare your case and a solicitor or barrister to appear for you in court. It is particularly important that you should obtain legal aid if possible for county court proceedings. The proceedings are more formal than an industrial tribunal hearing and it is more difficult to conduct your own case. Furthermore, if you are not legally aided and you lose your case, even if you had reasonable grounds for bringing it, you will normally be ordered to pay the defendent's costs, which could be substantial if he has been represented by a solicitor or barrister. Legal aid is not available for industrial tribunal hearings.

Whatever kind of complaint you have, there are several other places to which you can go for help in preparing or presenting your case. The Commission for Racial Equality has the power to help you. The help given could take the form of initial advice, an attempt to negotiate a settlement of your claim or even representation at the hearing by a solicitor or barrister or a complaints officer from the Commission. The addresses of the Commission offices are set out in the Appendix at the back of this book. The Commission will not always be able to provide representation at the hearing of your case, because its funds are limited, but you will at least normally be able to obtain initial advice from the Commission.

Whatever kind of case it is, you may be able to obtain some free advice from a solicitor under what is known as the "green form" scheme. Right at the start you can find out whether the advice will be free or, if not, how much you will have to pay, by giving the solicitor details of your income, savings and dependants.

You may also be able to obtain free advice and even representation at the hearing from your trade union, if you belong to one, or at a Law Centre. You could also go along to your local Citizen's Advice Bureau or Community Relations Officer in order to discuss your case informally and find out the best place to go to for more detailed advice and assistance. Your local CRO may even be prepared to take on your case and to represent you at a tribunal hearing.

It is very important that you should start looking for expert help and advice as soon as you know that you could have a claim and not wait until you have actually started proceedings and the date has been fixed for the hearing.

Settlement of your claim

Most cases which actually reach an industrial tribunal fail, even where the claimant is legally represented. This does not, however, necessarily mean that you are unlikely to obtain any compensation or other satisfaction for any discrimination against you. Many people who bring a case of racial discrimination or threaten to do so are able to negotiate a satisfactory settlement of their claim.

If your claim is in the employment field you will be able to use the services of an ACAS conciliation officer to try to settle your claim. The conciliation officer will discuss your claim both with you and with the employer or other party against whom you have brought the complaint. If no settlement can be achieved and your case is heard by a tribunal nothing which you have said to the conciliation officer can be used against you at the hearing.

The questionnaire procedure

We shall see examples in later chapters of a very important procedure which is available whatever kind of complaint you have. This is a procedure under which before you actually start proceedings (or, in employment cases, either before starting proceedings or within three weeks after starting them), you can send a questionnaire to the other party asking for relevant information. The replies given to the questionnaire may help to show you whether you have a good claim. If the other party refuses to answer or gives evasive or dishonest answers this can be held against him at the court or tribunal hearing.

Documents

Quite often, in order to prove your claim, you will need to ask for relevant documents to be produced. A request for production of the documents must be made to the other party well before the hearing and, if necessary, the court or tribunal can be asked before the hearing to make an order for the documents to be produced. It has been ruled by the House of Lords* that the court or tribunal should order the production of documents which are necessary to do justice to your case even though the documents are confidential documents.

Appeals

Whether you win or lose your case, there is a right of appeal on a point of law. Appeals from the industrial tribunals go to the Employment Appeal Tribunal and there can sometimes be a further appeal to the Court of Appeal. Appeals from the county court go direct to the Court of Appeal. Very occasionally, in both employment cases and other cases, there can be a further appeal from the Court of Appeal to the House of Lords.

Cases

In order to take your case to a court or tribunal it is not necessary to know very much about previous decisions of the courts. An industrial tribunal is not concerned with rulings made by other industrial tribunals and county court judges do not have to follow rulings made by other county court judges. The only rules of law which have to be followed are those laid down by the Appeal Courts and Tribunals. In this book a note will be given of only a handful of important appeal decisions which have laid down general principles.

The judges have stressed that it is important that industrial tribunals in particular should not become too bogged down in technicality and in detailed interpretation of appeal decisions. The tribunals are meant to be places where workers and employers can if they wish present their own cases and should not become a happy hunting ground for lawyers.

Chapter Summaries

At the end of some of the longer and more complicated chapters in this

---

* Science Research Council v. Nassé [1979] 3 All England Reports 673.

book, mainly in Part I, you will find summaries of the most important points mentioned in the chapter.

"Black", "coloured" etc

When giving examples of discrimination it is difficult to find a terminology which can be generally applicable. For example the word "black" is a word which you may use to describe yourself if you are of West Indian or African origin but not if you are of Asian origin. The word "coloured" is one which you may well not use to describe yourself if you are black. "Member of an ethnic minority group" is a clumsy term. I have accordingly throughout the book used terms like "black" and "coloured" fairly loosely. I have also used expressions such as "of Indian origin" to include both those born in India and those whose parents or other ancestors were from India and the expression "of Asian origin" to include all people who have come or whose parents or other ancestors have come from the Indian sub-continent.

Why do we need a Race Relations Act?

The purpose of this book is to explain the law, not to criticise it or defend it. However, I propose to state briefly some of the main reasons for having a Race Relations Act.

Racial discrimination is not the only kind of discrimination. Men and women are turned down for jobs because they speak with the wrong accent, went to the wrong school or play the wrong sport. Homosexuals, elderly people and the disabled often face discrimination. Why should discrimination against them be lawful and racial discrimination not be?

Racial discrimination, especially discrimination on the ground of colour, is particularly objectionable for three reasons. First, there is no rational basis for it, because your colour can have nothing to do with, say, your ability to do a job well. Secondly, there is nothing you can do to change your colour, even if you want to. Thirdly, you are an easy target for those minded to discriminate because your colour makes you stand out.

It is not only because racial discrimination is obnoxious that Parliament has acted against it. There was also the question of the scale of the problem. If there had been only a few thousand black and brown people living in Great Britain and if they had only occasionally faced discrimination then the Race Relations Act would not have been passed. However, there are not a few thousand, but a couple of million, black and brown people living in the country, most of them British citizens and around half of them born here. When the first Race Relations Act was passed, in 1965, racial discrimination occurred on a wide scale, often quite openly.

Moreover many black and brown people have difficulties enough without having to face racial discrimination as well. If you have a black or brown skin, the chances are that either you or your parents were born overseas. English may once have been a foreign language to you. Your education may have been interrupted. If you face further obstacles because of something as irrelevant as the colour of your skin, it is even more difficult for you to fulfil your potential as a member of the community.

But did we really need a law against discrimination? Should not the problem have been solved by educating people not to be prejudiced? This argument has its attractions. The objection to it is that the process of education would have taken many years during which hundreds of thousands of British citizens would have been denied any real equality of opportunity.

But is not the law an infringement of individual freedom? Yes, it is to some extent. The individual who owns a business for example no longer has the absolute freedom to decide whom he should employ or sell his goods to. He has been compulsorily liberated from his prejudices. But the Race Relations Act is only one of many fetters to have been placed on his freedom of action, in this age of consumer legislation.

In any case, it would be wrong to place too much emphasis on the question of freedom. Before we had laws against discrimination, many people discriminated because they thought that their employees or customers expected them to do so. They regarded themselves as being personally free from racial prejudice, but deferred to the real or imagined prejudices of others. It has required legislation to counteract their fears that by not discriminating they could have lost business or caused unrest amongst their employees.

Moreover, not all jobs are handed out by the *owners* of businesses. Many people work in local government or the civil service or public bodies. The public servants who do the hiring and firing in the public sector owe a duty to the public to act in a responsible way and to make sure that the best applicant is chosen for any job. They are not entitled to indulge their private prejudices at the expense of people who apply for jobs or who work under them.

Finally, has the law been a success? The law should not be judged simply on the number of successful cases of racial discrimination. The law has an important declaratory effect by laying down the standards which employers and others should observe. Many employers and others who would once have discriminated no longer do so, not because they are afraid of having to pay compensation but because they believe in obeying the law.

Summary

1. There is direct discrimination against you if (a) you are treated unfavourably and (b) this is on racial grounds – ie. on grounds of colour, nationality, race or ethnic or national origins.
2. Victimisation, which has the same consequences as direct racial discrimination, happens when you are treated unfavourably because you have, for example, made a claim under the Race Relations Act or given evidence for some other person making a claim. But there is victimisation for the purposes of the Act only if you have acted in good faith in making your claim or giving evidence.
3. The question of indirect discrimination arises if:
   (a) A requirement or condition has been applied to you.
   (b) You cannot comply with it.
   (c) Being unable to comply with it is to your disadvantage (eg. because it has ruled you out of consideration for a job).
   (d) The proportion of the relevant members of your racial group who cannot comply with the requirement is considerably greater than the proportion of the relevant non-members of the

group who cannot comply with it.

The person against whom you are complaining can still defeat your claim by proving that the requirement or condition is justifiable. Even if the requirement or condition is not proved to be justifiable, you will not be entitled to any compensation if it can be shown that the requirement or condition was not racially motivated.

4. The Race Relations Act gives you a right not to be discriminated against both when you are applying for jobs and when you are at work. You have rights not only against employers but also against other people and bodies in the employment field, such as employment agencies, trade unions and training bodies. Outside the employment field you have rights in respect of housing, education and goods, facilities and services which are provided to members of the public.

5. There are several exceptions to the rights which the Act gives you. For example you cannot do anything about any racial discrimination which is authorised by an Act of Parliament, a statutory regulation or the Immigration Rules.

6. Complaints about discrimination in the employment field are heard by industrial tribunals. The form applying to have your case heard by a tribunal must be received at the tribunal office within three months after the act of discrimination which you are complaining about. Any claim about discrimination outside the employment field is heard by a county court judge. Proceedings must be commenced within six months after the act of discrimination (subject to an extension of two months where you have applied to the Commission for Racial Equality for assistance).

Part I

Looking for work

This part contains five chapters. Chapter 1 sets out your rights when applying for a job. It also shows how other people, as well as employers, are forbidden to discriminate against you when you are looking for work, vocational training, a job qualification or trade union membership.

Chapter 2 explains the few occasions on which employers and others are allowed to discriminate against you when you are applying for a job.

Chapter 3 gives examples of some of the forms that direct discrimination takes and some tips on how you can recognise racial discrimination and later on prove to an industrial tribunal that you have been the victim of discrimination.

Chapter 4 gives examples of the main kinds of indirect discrimination which you may meet. It also explains why, even when the facts are not in doubt, it is sometimes impossible to say in advance whether your claim will succeed.

Finally, Chapter 5 contains practical advice for you if you think that you may have suffered either from direct or indirect discrimination (or victimisation).

1

Your rights against employers and others

Rights against employers

The general rule, to which there are few exceptions, is that no employer may discriminate against you, directly or indirectly, when you apply for a job. It does not matter whether the employer has a tiny business, with no existing staff, or whether the employer is a massive public company or government department. You are entitled to have your job application considered without any racial discrimination whenever you are looking for work at an office, factory, shop or other establishment in England, Wales or Scotland (or, generally, on a British ship or aircraft). You have this right whatever your colour, race or national or ethnic origin. You have the same right even if you are not a British citizen or not permanently settled in Great Britain, provided that you have a work permit or do not need one.

When your application for a job fails, it can happen in one of many ways. For example you write in answer to an advertisement and are either refused an interview or hear nothing at all; you telephone about a job which has been advertised and are told that the job has already been filled; you call at a factory on the off-chance that there is work available and are told that there are no vacancies; you are interviewed and then receive a letter telling you that somebody else has been given the job; you are interviewed and the employer then appoints somebody else or leaves the job vacant without letting you know at all. The law forbids employers to treat you in any of these ways if in so doing they are directly or indirectly discriminating against you.

You could have a claim against an employer even if you are offered a job for which you have applied. There must be no discrimination by employers in fixing the wage or other terms of employment offered to you. For example:

i You are offered a job for which you have applied. The employer believes that because you are black you will have difficulty in finding any alternative job. He therefore offers you less than the advertised wage. In doing so he is directly discriminating against you contrary to the Race Relations Act

Discrimination by employees

If you suffer racial discrimination when you apply for a job, this is not always at the hands of the employer himself. Many employers, especially large organisations, employ personnel officers and heads of department to take on staff. Sometimes you may even get no further than a doorman or receptionist who tells you that there are no vacancies. Can the employer escape liability if it is some employee who has been discriminating on his behalf? If so, can you take action against the individual who has discriminated against you?

You will usually have a claim against both the employer and the person who has actually discriminated against you. The employer can escape liability only by showing that he has taken all reasonably practicable steps to stop this sort of discrimination happening. If the employer can show that all such steps have been taken then your only claim is against the offending individual, but it rarely happens in practice that employers are able to succeed in this defence. For example:

ii You ring up about a vacancy for a typist. The receptionist can tell by your accent and your name that you are of Asian origin and because she is prejudiced she falsely tells you that the job has already been taken. Two years ago the firm decided to adopt an equal opportunity policy and told all their staff about it, but since then they have done nothing at all to make sure that the policy is being put into effect. You would have a claim against both the receptionist and against the employer.

Self-employed contractors

You can have a claim under the Race Relations Act even when you apply for work to a person who would not technically be your employer if you got the job. For example:

iii   You are of West Indian origin and you apply for a job as a sales representative. All the representatives who work for the firm are technically self-employed and are paid on a commission basis. You are turned down because you are black. This racial discrimination against you is unlawful.

Contract workers

The same rule applies if you are discriminated against when you turn up to do work as a temp or some other kind of contract work. For example:

iv   You are a typist of West African origin and you are employed as a temp by an agency. You are sent along to an office to spend a week working as the secretary to one of the partners whose own secretary is on holiday. Because of your colour he tells the agency to send another typist in your place. You have a claim against him.

Employment Agencies

Sometimes you apply for work not directly to an employer but through a jobcentre or some other public or private employment agency. You will have a claim against any employment agency which discriminates against you and you could also have a claim against the employer. For example:

v   You are of Asian origin. An employment agency has advertised a vacancy in a workshop and you ask about this job. Unknown to you, the employer has told the agency that no coloured applicants will be acceptable and the agency falsely tells you that the job has been taken. You find out about this because a white friend of yours applies for the same job and is offered an interview. You have a claim against both the agency and the employer.

It is not only when you are applying for some particular job that employment agencies must not discriminate against you. If it is part of the function of the agency to help you to find work or to give you careers advice there must be no discrimination by the agency either in refusing to provide either of those services to you or in the way in which the services are provided. The agency must not discriminate either in the terms on which it offers to provide any of its services. For example:

vi   You are a typist of West Indian origin. You ask a private secretarial agency to put you on their books to try to find work for you. They charge you a higher fee than their normal fee. They tell you that because you are black it will be harder for them to find work for you and therefore it is reasonable for them to ask a higher fee. This direct racial discrimination against you is unlawful.

Training bodies

Sometimes, in order to obtain work, you will need vocational training. Training bodies include public bodies, such as the Manpower Services Commission, and private associations set up by employers to provide training for their employees. Sometimes a training body runs a training course itself and sometimes it sponsors places on a training course run by somebody else. There must be no direct or indirect racial discrimination against you by a training body in refusing you a place on a training course or refusing to sponsor you for a training course. In Chapter 4 we shall see an example of a case of indirect discrimination against a training body, although in that particular case the training body's requirement was held to be justifiable and the claim failed.

Qualifying bodies

A qualifying body is any authority or body which can give you some kind of qualification or licence to enable you to work at your trade or profession. Sometimes the qualification or licence is essential; sometimes it is useful but not essential. In the legal profession, for example, you cannot take a job as a solicitor unless you have a practising certificate from the Law Society. You can take a job as a legal executive without any licence or qualification, but it may help you to obtain a job if you are a Fellow of the Institute of Legal Executives. Both the Law Society and the Institute of Legal Executives are qualifying bodies for the purposes of the Race Relations Act.

A qualifying body which has the power to grant a licence or qualification to you must not discriminate against you by refusing it; in the terms on which it is offered to you; by subsequently withdrawing it from you; or by varying the terms on which you hold it.

Trade unions

There are many jobs where it is necessary or useful for you to be a member of a trade union. There must be no discrimination by a trade union either in refusing your application for membership or in the terms on which you are offered membership. It can never be a defence to an act of direct discrimination for the trade union to show that the discrimination was designed to protect the interests of its existing members. For example:

vii   You are a foreign national. You have a work permit to take up a job in this country. You apply to join the trade union to which all the workers at the establishment belong. Your application is refused in retaliation against the trade unions in your own country, who have made it impossible for British workers to obtain jobs there. This racial discrimination against you, however understandable, is unlawful.

Summary of Chapter 1

1. The general rule is that no employer may discriminate against you in refusing or ignoring your application for a job.
2. If an employee, such as a personnel officer, discriminates on behalf of the employer in turning down your application, then you will usually have a claim against both the employer and the employee.
3. You may have a claim against somebody for whom you wish to do work, even if you are not their employee in the strict sense of the word, but a contract worker or someone who is technically self-employed.

27

4. If an employment agency discriminates against you you will have a claim against the agency and you may also have a claim against the employer on whose behalf the agency was discriminating.

5. You also have a right not to be discriminated against by vocational training bodies, qualifying bodies and trade unions.

2

Exceptions – when the law permits discrimination against you

Occasionally, if you meet racial discrimination when applying for a job, you may be able to do nothing about it. Sometimes (but not always) racial discrimination against you is permitted if you are applying for a job as a domestic servant, a waiter, an actor or model, a social worker or a civil servant or if you are applying to join the armed forces.

Private households

The widest of these exceptions is for domestic employment. When you are applying for a job in a private household the employer may freely turn you down because of your colour or on some other racial ground. It may surprise you to learn this, because you may from time to time have read that householders who advertise in the newspaper, for example for a "Scots cook", are breaking the law. The explanation is as follows. Any householder who is looking for staff to work in his or her household may freely discriminate. Accordingly, if you apply for a job as a household cook or maid or if you wish to work at a large house as the gardener or chauffeur you cannot complain if you are turned down because of the colour of your skin or on some other racial ground.

However, the householder must not state his or her racial preferences when advertising the job. The reason is that members of ethnic minority groups would find it offensive if they were constantly opening their newspapers and seeing advertisements stating that coloured applicants for jobs would not be acceptable. If you see such an advertisement and are upset or offended by it there is nothing that you personally can do except report the facts to the Commission for Racial Equality. Only the Commission has the power to take action against the offending employer.

All this does not mean that if you are a coloured cook or gardener or maid or chauffeur you can never apply for a job without the risk of facing racial discrimination and being able to do nothing about it. The discrimination is lawful only if the job is one for the purposes of a private household. You will have grounds for a complaint to an industrial tribunal if you meet racial discrimination when you apply for a job as a cook in a works canteen or restaurant, when you apply for a job as a company chauffeur, when you apply for a job as a gardener at a school or in a park, or when you apply for a job as a maid at a hotel.

There are two ways in which you could have a claim even if you are denied the chance to work in a private household. First of all, the exception does not apply if you are a temp or some other kind of contract worker. For example:

i   Your parents were from Pakistan. You have previously applied for a job as a household cook and been turned down because of your colour. You are now working for an agency and are sent along as a temp to the very same household. You would have a claim against the house owner if he refused to let you do the job.

Secondly, there must be no discrimination against you by way of victimisation, even when you are applying for a job in a private household. For example:

ii   You are of West Indian origin. You apply for a job as a cook at a private house. You had previously been employed at the householder's factory and you left that job after complaining about racial discrimination and successfully taking your case to an industrial tribunal. The householder now refuses to employ you not because you are West Indian but because he regards you as a troublemaker. This discrimination against you is not permitted by the Act.

The civil service and armed forces

There is a general rule under the Race Relations Act that any racial discrimination is lawful if it is expressly authorised by some Act of Parliament or statutory regulation. There are also more specific provisions relating to jobs in the civil service and applications to join the armed forces. If the rules governing entry to the civil service or the armed forces restrict admission on grounds of birth, nationality, descent or residence and if you do not qualify under those rules then there is nothing you can do about it. For example, if you are a foreign national (and not Irish) then you will probably not be eligible for a post in the civil service. Even if you are a British citizen, there will be some posts which are not open to you if you or one of your parents was born overseas. For example, the Ministry of Defence has particularly strict entry requirements.

However, there must be no direct discrimination on grounds of colour. If you are a coloured British citizen and you are eligible in all respects for a post in the civil service or a place in the armed forces then you can complain to an industrial tribunal if you are turned down because of your colour.

Professional sportsmen

There are one or two other jobs where direct discrimination against you on grounds of colour is forbidden but other kinds of racial discrimination are allowed. If you apply for a job as a professional sportsman to represent a particular area, then you can lawfully be turned down because of your place of birth or your nationality or because you have not lived long enough in the area. For example, if you are a professional cricketer and want to play county cricket the county to which you apply for a job could either turn you down out of hand if you were born outside the county or could make you wait until you have qualified to play for the county by living there for a specified period. However, the county could not lawfully refuse to employ you just because of the colour of your skin.

Charities

It is also very occasionally possible that you may face lawful racial discrimination if you apply for work to a charity which makes work available as part of its charitable function. For example:

iii   You are a disabled Englishman and you apply for a place at a workshop for disabled people. However, when that workshop was set up one of the terms of the trust was that it should provide work for disabled people born in Scotland. You could lawfully be refused a place on this ground. However, if you were a coloured Scotsman you could not be refused work on the ground of your colour, even if the trust deed stipulated white people.

Statutory officers

You have no claim under the Race Relations Act if the job which you are denied is a statutory office, paid or unpaid. A statutory office is an office in the public service which is created by statute. Statutory officers include Ministers of the Crown, Justices of the Peace and Judges. For example:

iv   You are white. You have been hoping for a long time to be appointed a Justice of the Peace. A new batch of persons appointed includes several Asians, because the Asian community is felt to be unrepresented on the local bench, and you are left out. You can have no claim under the Race Relations Act.

There is one kind of statutory office to which the exception does not apply. A police officer is a statutory officer but the Act expressly provides that the office of constable is to be treated as employment. Accordingly, you could have a claim under the Act if there is racial discrimination against you when you apply to join the police force.

Waiters and entertainers

The rules relating to sportsmen, charities and statutory officers are not of great general practical importance. Rather more attention needs to be paid to two lawful excuses which employers can have for restricting a job to applicants of a particular ethnic background. One of these is where the job is in catering or entertainment or modelling and it is reasonable in the interests of authenticity that the field of applicants should be limited to members of a particular racial group. For example:

v   You are a white drummer. You apply unsuccessfully for a job in a steel band which contains only West Indian members. It is unlikely that any claim of racial discrimination would be upheld.

vi   You are black and you apply for a job as a waiter at a Chinese restaurant. At this restaurant only Chinese food is served and all the waiters are of Chinese origin so as to create an oriental atmosphere. You can have no complaint if your application for the job is turned down. However, if you had been a cook and you had applied for a job which would have required you to be in the kitchens all the time, so that the customers would never actually have seen you, the restaurant owner could not lawfully turn you down on the ground that he wanted a cook of Chinese origin.

Even in the entertainment field there are limits to the exception for authenticity. Because the character being portrayed in a film or play is of a particular colour or national origin it does not always mean that the actor playing that part has to be of the same colour or national origin. It is not usual to insist on a Dane to play Hamlet, an Egyptian to play Cleopatra or a Moor to play Othello.

Social workers, etc

The term used by the law when jobs can lawfully be restricted to applicants of a particular ethnic background is that being of that background is a genuine occupational qualification for the job. The other occasion when this can happen is where the job will involve you in providing members of a particular racial group with personal services promoting their welfare and those services can most effectively be provided by a member of the same group. For example:

vii   You are a social worker of West African origin. You apply to a local authority for a job as a social worker. There is in the town a large community of people who came to England from Bangladesh and many of the women do not speak English and do not often leave the house. One of the duties of the job for which you are applying will be to help these women to overcome any difficulties and to play a full part in the life of the community. It would probably be lawful for the council to refuse your application for the job and insist on appointing a social worker who is also of Bangladeshi origin. However, if the council already has on its staff a social worker from Bangladesh it must first of all consider whether the work load of the department can be re-arranged so as to give to the existing social worker the job of helping the women from Bangladesh so that the new job can be opened up to applicants of any ethnic background.

The industrial tribunals would not allow employers to abuse this genuine occupational qualification rule by using it as a cloak for straightforward racial discrimination. For example:

viii You are a personnel officer born in India and you apply for a job at a factory. The factory owner tells you that all the workers at the factory are white and were born in England and that they would respond much better to a personnel officer who was also born in England. Your application is therefore turned down. This discrimination against you is clearly unlawful.

Employers cannot use the genuine occupational qualification exception outside the areas of catering, entertainment, modelling and personnel and social work. However good the commercial motive may be, an employer is not allowed to decide for himself that a job is suitable only for members of a particular ethnic background. For example:

ix   You are a Jew and you apply for a job as an export sales manager. You would be working mainly in this country but the job would involve annual visits to a large customer in an Arab country. The employer cannot lawfully turn down your application on the ground that a Jewish sales representative would be unacceptable to the Arab customer.

x   Your parents came from Pakistan. You apply for a job on a particular shift in a factory. You are more suitable in other respects than an applicant from India, but he gets the job because the other workers on the shift are of Indian origin and the factory owner thinks that he will get on better with them. This racial discrimination against you is unlawful.

Positive discrimination

It does not make any difference if the racial discrimination is for reasons which are benevolent rather than commercial. For example:

xi   You apply for a job as a chief officer with a local authority. You are white. The council has decided as a matter of policy that only coloured applicants will be considered, because all the existing chief officers employed by the council are white. If you are refused an interview because you are white the council is in breach of the Race Relations Act.

An employer who wishes to discriminate positively cannot lawfully do so simply by relaxing the job requirements in favour of ethnic minority applicants. For example:

xii   You are white. You apply for a job and are turned down because you have only three 'O' levels. The employer requires applicants to have at least five 'O' levels. However, the employer appoints a black applicant who, like you, has only three 'O' levels. The employer has directly discriminated against you, contrary to the Act, by requiring you to meet a higher standard because you are white. It would have been lawful for the employer to relax the entry requirements for all applicants and to regard 'O' levels as only one of several factors to be taken into account, so that otherwise outstanding applicants, of whatever colour, who did not have the five 'O' levels could be considered for the job.

It is arguable (but by no means certain) that the discrimination against you in the above example would have been lawful if the job for which you applied were a job as a trainee. This is because of the general exception in the Act permitting discrimination in the provision of facilities or services to meet the special needs of members of a racial group in regard to their education, training or welfare.

Training bodies

Although there must in general be no positive discrimination by employers, there is a special exception for training bodies. If it seems to a training body that at any time during the previous twelve months, proportionately few of the members of a racial group were doing some particular work, either in Great Britain as a whole or in the area where the work is to be carried out, then the training body can lawfully discriminate in favour of a member of that racial group in giving or sponsoring places on a training course. For example:

xiii   You are white. You apply for a place on a training course to become a computer programmer. You are unsuccessful, because a number of places on the course have been specially reserved for West Indian applicants. It appears to the training body that the proportion of computer programmers in Great Britain who are West Indian is small compared with the proportion of the population who are West Indian. The discrimination against you is lawful.

Workers from overseas

The Race Relations Act only applies to jobs at establishments in Great Britain (and on most British ships and aircraft). There is also a special provision in the Act relating to the provision of education or training for people who do not live in Great Britain and who intend to leave the country after their education or training. For example:

xiv   You apply for a job as a trainee at a factory. The company has an associate company in France. The job has been reserved for a trainee from the French factory who will come over to take the job and then return to France when he has completed his training. The discrimination against you is lawful.

Summary of Chapter 2

1. There are very few exceptions to the general rule that employers must not discriminate against you when you are applying for a job.
2. The main exception is that discrimination is usually permitted when you are seeking to be employed for the purposes of a private household.
3. There are special restrictions covering entry to the civil service and armed forces, but even here direct discrimination on the ground of colour is against the law.
4. There are a few, but only a few, jobs in entertainment, catering, modelling and social and personnel work which may on occasion be lawfully restricted to members of a particular racial group.
5. There are exceptions, of little general importance, relating to

statutory officers, sportsmen, jobs provided by charities and trainees from overseas.

6. Positive discrimination by an employer in turning down your application for a job is almost always unlawful, but positive discrimination by training bodies is generally permitted.

Recognising and proving direct discrimination

Your application for a job has been turned down or ignored. Has there been direct racial discrimination against you? You will often find it very difficult to answer this question. If your application for an interview is refused or ignored, how are you to know the reason? You have probably never met the employer and may know nothing about him. Even if you are turned down after an interview, it is difficult after only a short meeting with the employer to know whether a reason given for turning down your application is genuine or an excuse for discrimination.

In this chapter, we shall look at some of the ways in which employers who discriminate against you could give themselves away. There are four general points which you should bear in mind.

First, you must guard against seeing racial discrimination where none in fact exists. In a time of high unemployment you may apply for many jobs without success. Even when an employer behaves badly, by ignoring your application for a job or failing to write to you as promised after an interview, this is not necessarily evidence of racial discrimination. Unfortunately breaking promises and showing a lack of consideration are not uncommon faults.

Secondly, following on from this, you must be careful not to go into job interviews obviously on the lookout for discrimination against you. A successful interview depends on a good relationship being established between you and the employer and you are not going to be able to create that sort of relationship if you go in expecting to meet discrimination and ready to pounce on any insensitive remark by the interviewer.

Thirdly, what if you do meet discrimination? Suppose for example, that an employer or personnel officer has said something to you on the telephone or at an interview that has convinced you that he is prejudiced against you. At the earliest opportunity write down exactly what was said as fully as you can remember it. Write down the exact words used. Write down everything that you can remember and not just the offending remarks. Write down your side of the conversation as well. Look at your notes afterwards to see if there was anything that you said which could have led the employer or personnel officer genuinely to think that you were unqualified or otherwise unsuitable for the job.

Fourthly, do not despair if the evidence which you have of discrimination does not appear to be absolutely conclusive. There is a very useful method by which you can look for extra evidence. This involves sending to the employer the form of questionnaire which has already been mentioned in the Introduction to this book. The ways in which the form can be useful are considered towards the end of this chapter.

Admitted discrimination

Before you reach the questionnaire stage, what kind of evidence of discrimination are you likely to obtain? You may think that no employer would ever be so insensitive and so ignorant or defiant of the law as to admit that he is turning you down because of your colour or on some other racial ground. However, you may still meet the sort of employer who thinks that he is permitted to discriminate so long as it is not because he is personally prejudiced. For example:

i   You are Irish and you apply for a job in a small garage. The garage owner says that he would like to take you on but his other mechanic is very hostile to the Irish and would give you a hard time. He thinks it better therefore that you should look elsewhere.

Sometimes an employer discriminates because of real or supposed prejudice by customers rather than by existing employees. For example:

ii   You are of Pakistani origin. You apply for a job as a sales representative, visiting customers at their homes. The sales manager who interviews you tells you that he would like to give you the job, but that you would be likely to meet a lot of prejudice from customers and this would be embarrassing for you and could also lose sales for the company. Because of this he is not prepared to offer you the job.

In both the above examples the discrimination against you is unlawful. An employer cannot justify racial discrimination by showing that his existing employees or customers are prejudiced, even if he can prove that by taking you on he would lose customers. For example:

iii   You are of black African origin. You apply for a job as a works manager. The main customer of the company is a South African firm which regularly sends representatives over to look round the factory. You are turned down for the job because the South African customers would not like to have you showing them round the factory. This discrimination against you is unlawful.

If you are told, at an interview or when you telephone, that you cannot have the job because of your colour or origin, does it matter that there is no witness to the conversation? Would it be a waste of time for you to take your case to an industrial tribunal knowing that the employer may deny what he has said to you and that it would then be your word against his. It is for you to prove your case and satisfy the tribunal that discrimination has occurred, but it is possible to win a case on your evidence alone even without obtaining extra evidence using the questionnaire procedure. So long as the tribunal believe your evidence and are not convinced by the evidence given by the employer they will find in your favour. It does help though if you can obtain additional evidence. The following example is based on an actual case:

iv   You are white. You apply for a job in an office having had several years' experience in similar jobs. You are interviewed by the company chairman who makes disparaging remarks about black people, says that the only other applicant, a West Indian, will be interviewed as a formality and offers you the job. You then explain that your husband is West Indian. The chairman says that he will telephone you later about the job but fails to do so. When you telephone the company you are told that the job has been given to somebody else. It turns out that this is a white girl without adequate experience. The fact that a less experienced person has been appointed supports your own evidence of the interview.

The above example is rather unusual because the discrimination was not on the ground of your colour but on the ground of your husband's colour. The law gives an employer no more right to turn you down for a job because of your husband's or wife's colour than to turn you down because of your own colour.

Sometimes the employer may quite openly discriminate against you because he wrongly believes that the discrimination is lawful. For example:

v   You are white. You apply for a job as a chef at a Chinese restaurant. The job would involve working entirely in the kitchen and you would never be seen by the customers. The restaurant owner does not realise that it is only when taking on waiters and other staff who would be on show that he is sometimes permitted to discriminate in order to preserve the atmosphere of the restaurant. He turns you down for the job and at the industrial tribunal hearing tries to argue that he was entitled to do so. You should win your case without any difficulty.

Admissions made to third parties

Sometimes an employer will say to some third party what he would hesitate to say to your face. This could often happen when you apply for a job through a jobcentre or private employment agency. For example:

vi   You are of Indian origin. You go along to a secretarial agency and the interviewer from the agency telephones an employer. The employer has a vacancy and the interviewer arranges to send you along to see him. However, when the interviewer tells the employer your name the employer immediately says that he does not wish to employ any Asian people and that he is not willing to see you. You are able to guess from the interviewer's side of the conversation what was happening and when you ask her the interviewer tells you exactly what the employer said.

If in the above example you wish to bring a claim of racial

crimination against the employer you will need the evidence of tne interviewer from the employment agency. You should ask her both for the name and address of the employer she spoke to and also for her own name and address. You should also ask her there and then if she would be willing to give evidence on your behalf and ask her to let you have a written statement. If she says that she is reluctant to get involved because the agency may not like it you should point out that there are provisions in the Race Relations Act to prevent a person being victimised for giving evidence in a racial discrimination case. Anyway the agency may well be glad for her to give evidence on your behalf because the agency would not come well out of any proceedings if it appeared to be conniving at discrimination by employers.

You should also seriously consider going along right away to the office of the man to whom the interviewer has just spoken to or at least telephoning him to say that you would like to be interviewed for the job. If you speak to him, or even to his secretary, and are told that he is not willing to see you, then you will have your own evidence to add to that of the interviewer from the employment agency.

What you must not do is take your case to the industrial tribunal with nothing more than your evidence of what the interviewer from the employment agency has told you the employer said to her. Without the interviewer as a witness or obtaining your own first hand evidence by speaking to the employer personally you cannot hope to prove that discrimination has occurred.

False reason for rejection

When an employer does not openly admit that he is discriminating against you, the strongest evidence of discrimination is usually that the employer has given a false reason for turning you down and that you can show the reason to be false. For example:

vii   You are of Asian origin. You see a vacancy advertised for a job as a receptionist and you telephone the employer. The employer at first offers you an interview but when you tell him your name, which is a common Indian name, he says that on second thoughts he is not prepared to interview you because he already has enough people to see. You use the questionnaire procedure and ask why you were refused an interview. The reply is that the job of a receptionist required someone who spoke English well. In fact you speak perfect English, as the members of the tribunal see for themselves when you give evidence.

The members of the tribunal could regard it as being sufficient proof of racial discrimination that the employer has given a reason which they can see to be totally false. However, it is important to remember that if an employer turns you down for a reason which he believes to be true then you cannot prove that he is really discriminating just by showing that he was wrong in his belief. For example:

viii You are of West Indian origin. You apply for a job in a factory which is several miles away from your home. It would be difficult to travel from your home to the factory by public transport. The works manager who interviews you asks if you have your own car. You reply that you do not have a car and forget to tell him that you have a motorbike. He gives the job to another applicant who has less experience than you but who lives nearer the factory. When you ask him why you have not been offered the job he tells you that it is because you would have difficulty in getting to work on time. It is no good taking the case to an industrial tribunal and telling the tribunal that you could have got to work on time because you have a motorbike. The person whom you should have told was the works manager.

One of the common reasons which employers give for turning down applications for jobs is that the vacancy has already been filled. This could happen to you in several ways. You may write or telephone in answer to an application and be told that the appointment has already been made. You may turn up casually at the factory looking for work and be told that there are no vacancies. You may even be interviewed and then receive a letter saying that one of the other applicants has been appointed. If you can show that the vacancy still existed when the statement was made to you then the industrial tribunal may be willing to accept that the real reason why you were turned down was your colour or ethnic origin.

The following example is based on an actual case:

ix You are a black Jamaican. You apply for a job in a factory in response to a newspaper advertisement. You are interviewed by the works manager who says that he will let you know. You do not hear anything and when you telephone the company several times you are told each time that the vacancy has been filled. However, the advertisement for the job keeps appearing in the local paper.

In the above example you would have grounds for a claim. It is just possible that the company may have taken on another applicant who is better qualified than you and that he may have failed to take up the job, leading to the further advertisements. However, you can find out by sending the form of questionnaire to the company and asking them for the name and address, date of appointment and qualifications and experience of the successful applicant.

Sometimes when you are told that a vacancy has been filled you can test the story by getting a friend of a different colour or ethnic origin to apply for the same job. Again the following example is based on an actual case:

x   You are of African origin. You apply for a job in a shop and are told that the vacancy has been filled. You arrange for a white friend to apply for the same job and your friend is offered the job.

In the above example it would be essential both for you and your white friend to give evidence. You should each write down as soon as possible exactly what was said to you by the shop manager in case it is suggested that there was some misunderstanding and that the manager did not tell you that the job was taken.

Questions at interview

What if the employer turns you down and the reason which he gives has nothing to do with your colour or any other racial ground and could be a genuine one? Is there any other way in which you can prove discrimination? It is no use bringing a claim if you simply have a feeling or impression that an interviewer may be prejudiced against you. An industrial tribunal will require more tangible evidence than that. Even evidence that the interviewer had a hostile and aggressive attitude will not usually be enough unless you can give specific examples of what he said and the way he said it. An industrial tribunal cannot make a finding of discrimination unless they are satisfied that you are right in the belief which you formed and you can only satisfy them by putting over to them exactly what the interview was like. This is why it is so important for you to make detailed notes as quickly as possible after the interview.

If you can satisfy the tribunal that the employer asked you a lot of questions which had nothing at all to do with the job then they may be willing to conclude that he was just going through the motions and never really intended to consider you seriously for the job. For example:

xi   You are of Indian origin. You apply for a skilled post in a laboratory. You have many years' experience of doing similar work. The head of research who interviews you asks you a few general questions about your hobbies but tells you nothing at all about the work involved in the job which you have applied for, asks you nothing about your previous experience and does not discuss at all the ways in which the new job could be different from your previous work.

It is possible that you would be able to convince an industrial tribunal that the man who interviewed you had already made his mind up not to appoint you and that this was because of your colour. However, you may find it difficult to win your case on this sort of evidence alone. Many interviewers ask strange questions not because they are racially prejudiced but because they are bad interviewers. Sometimes also questions which are apparently irrelevant are asked for a good reason.

You may also find it difficult to win a case simply by arguing that the questions which were put to you were themselves evidence of a prejudiced attitude of mind. For example:

xii   You were born in England but are of Indian origin. You apply for a job in a mill. The mill manager asks you if you will need extra long holidays in order to visit your relatives in India. You tell him that you have never been to India, that you have no close relatives there and that you have no intention of visiting India. The mill manager does not refer to the point again. It is unlikely that an industrial tribunal would take the view that merely by asking the question about travel to India the mill manager was revealing a prejudiced attitude of mind. It would be within the

.nowledge of the tribunal members that many West Indian and Asian workers do have relatives overseas and do from time to time ask for extended holidays in order to visit these relatives. It is legitimate for any prospective employer to explore any difficulties which could arise in this respect provided that this is done in a constructive way and not used simply as an excuse for turning down a job application.

It would have been different in the above example if the employer had refused to accept your answer and had kept coming back to the point and telling you about other Asian workers he had employed and who had taken unauthorised holidays. By persistent and repeated questioning he would have been indicating that he was not regarding you as an individual in your own right but simply lumping you together with the other Asians whom he had employed.

Similarly, if you are of Asian or West Indian origin and do not speak or understand English very well it is legitimate for a prospective employer to discuss with you whether your difficulty in communicating and understanding could cause practical problems, such as safety problems. So long as the employer looks at the matter in a constructive way, trying to find ways of overcoming any problems rather than looking for excuses to turn you down, an industrial tribunal would be unlikely to make a finding of racial discrimination simply because of the questions put to you. If on the other hand you speak perfect English and just because you are coloured the employer asks you if you have experienced any difficulties in making yourself understood the question is insulting and evidence of a prejudiced attitude.

The same goes for any questions which the employer asks you about racial prejudice itself. It is quite proper for an employer to discuss with you the possibility that you will face racial prejudice from other employees and customers, provided that he makes it clear that the company has an equal opportunity policy and tells you that if you get the job and meet prejudice then you will be entitled to look to him for support. If on the other hand an employer who turns you down for a job has discussed with you the question of racial prejudice and asked his questions in a way that makes it clear he shares the prejudice and expects you to prove him wrong, then the tribunal could regard his questions as being evidence of racial discrimination.

There is one general argument from employers which you may have to meet if you complain about being turned down for a job after you have been given an interview. The employer could argue that by offering you the interview in the first place the employer proved that there was no racial prejudice against you and that the eventual decision to turn you down was not racially motivated. This is not a very strong argument. An employer who is racially prejudiced may well take the view that by refusing even to interview a qualified candidate he could lay himself open immediately to a charge of racial discrimination. He decides therefore to go through the motions and to pretend to give you a fair deal by interviewing you.

Failure to reply to application

What if you do not even reach the interview stage and are never given any reason for the failure to offer you an interview? You write applying for a job and receive no reply at all. It is most unlikely that, without any further evidence, an industrial tribunal would make a finding of racial discrimination. Unfortunately it is all too common for employers simply to ignore job applications not because they are prejudiced but simply because they are lazy or discourteous. If you apply for a job which you are well qualified for and which you are very keen to have and receive no reply at all then, if you want to do anything about it, you should telephone the company to ask whether your application has been received and whether the company is willing to offer you an interview. If you are not to be offered an interview you should ask why. If, from the answers given to you, you have a suspicion that you may have been the victim of racial discrimination, then you should try to find out more by using the questionnaire procedure, always bearing in mind the time limit for taking proceedings (discussed in Chapter 5).

The questionnaire procedure

The following is an example of the way in which the questionnaire procedure could work in a case where you have nothing more than a n of discrimination:-

You are of West Indian origin. You apply in writing for a job for which you are well qualified. Your application is not even acknowledged. You telephone the company to ask whether you are going to be offered an interview. The person to whom you speak is very offhand and tells you that there were so many applicants it was not possible to interview all of them. You are surprised that in view of your first rate qualifications you have not even been offered an interview and you use the questionnaire procedure. In the questionnaire you ask, amongst other questions, why you were not offered an interview and you also ask for details of the qualifications and ethnic backgrounds of the applicants who were offered interviews. The answers to the questionnaire reveal that white applicants who were less qualified than you have been offered interviews. You therefore decide to take your case to an industrial tribunal. Although you cannot be sure to win your case, the information thrown up by the replies to the questionnaire calls for explanation and gives you reasonable grounds for taking your case to the tribunal.

In the above example, the value of the questionnaire procedure was to give you evidence of discrimination when you previously had no more than a suspicion. Sometimes the questionnaire helps because it strengthens evidence which you already have. For example:

xiv You are of Asian origin. You apply for an office job but are turned down after an interview. The interviewer asked you a number of questions which indicated a prejudiced attitude and after the interview you made a careful note of these questions. You use the questionnaire. You ask why you were not appointed and you also ask about the qualifications and experience of the successful applicant. The employer's reply reveals that the person offered the job was less experienced than you. No adequate reason for preferring that person to you is given. You therefore take your case to an industrial tribunal.

It is important to appreciate that you will not automatically win your case if you can prove that the person offered the job was less qualified or experienced than you. The members of the tribunal hearing your case are not there to decide whether the employer made the decision which they themselves would have made. They are there to decide whether you have proved that there has been direct racial discrimination. If the employer can satisfy them that there is a genuine explanation and that the decision was not taken on racial grounds then your claim will fail. However, the tribunal are likely to accept the choice of a less qualified or experienced applicant as being evidence of racial discrimination against you if no other explanation for the choice is given or if they do not believe the explanation given.

Sometimes the questionnaire procedure can be valuable because the information which you obtain stops you from carrying on with a hopeless case. For example:

xv   You are of Indian origin. You apply for a job for which you are well qualified. The interview goes well and the employer says that you are likely to be offered the job. Instead you receive a polite letter telling you that somebody else has been appointed. You use the questionnaire procedure. The reply states that the successful applicant, who was interviewed after you, was also of Indian origin. Accordingly you do not take your case any further.

Documents

In the above example, how can you be sure that the explanation given by the employer in the reply to the questionnaire is correct? What if an employer tries to fob you off with a lot of lies in his reply to your questionnaire? If you do not believe what has been told you by the employer and you press on with your case then you should be able to show whether the employer has been telling the truth or not. The reason is that you can insist on the employer producing at the hearing any documents which are necessary to your case, even if they are confidential documents. If you have had an interview for a job before being turned down then you can insist on production of your application and that of the successful applicant and also the notes of both interviews. If you have been refused an interview after making a written application for a job then you can require the production of your application and those received from all the applicants who were offered interviews. These documents will expose any false statements ᵉ employer in his reply to the questionnaire. The fact that ᴅde the false statements will tell very much against him at the ᴅl hearing.

ᴅ ᴅe way in which you should go about sending the questionnaire to the employer and asking for documents and the times at which these should be done are considered in Chapter 5.

Summary of Chapter 3

1. Even if you have no witnesses of discrimination and it is your word against the employer's a tribunal may nevertheless find in your favour if they believe your evidence, especially if the employer has admitted to you that he is turning you down on racial grounds or has given you a false reason for rejecting your application. Questions which indicate a prejudiced attitude may also sometimes be sufficient.

2. If the employer has admitted the discrimination to some other person, you should always arrange for that person to give evidence on your behalf at the tribunal hearing.

3. Sometimes a claim can be proved by the combined evidence of you and a friend of a different racial group, if the friend is offered a job after you have been told that the job has been taken.

4. Even if you have no more than a strong suspicion of discrimination, you may be able to obtain additional evidence by using the questionnaire procedure, especially when this shows that a less qualified and experienced person has been appointed.

4
Some common forms of indirect discrimination

The main purpose of this chapter is to look at some of the requirements and conditions by prospective employers which most commonly give rise to complaints of indirect discrimination. First of all there are a couple of general points.

The questionnaire

The questionnaire procedure which is available under the Race Relations Act was mentioned in the Introduction. Chapter 5 tells you where to get the form and when you must send it to the employer. If you wish to take a complaint of indirect discrimination to a tribunal hearing, the questionnaire may help you to find out what the main argument at the hearing will be about. For example:

i   You are from Pakistan. You do not speak English well. You ring up about a vacancy for a job. You are told by the employer that you cannot be considered for the job because you do not speak English well enough. You do not have anything in writing from the employer to confirm that you were turned down for this reason. You send the questionnaire to the employer. In answer to your questions the employer confirms that you were turned down because you could not comply with a requirement that you should be able to speak English well. You also ask whether the employer agrees that the proportion of Pakistanis who cannot comply with the requirement is considerably greater than the proportion of non-Pakistanis. This is a question which the employer may not be obliged to answer but he does and confirms that he agrees. All this is very useful, because it means that you ᴎot have to spend much time at the tribunal hearing on ᴊving that you were turned down because you could not ᴄomply with the requirement and that the requirement had a discriminatory effect. You would be able to come fairly quickly to the main issue, which would be whether the employer can show the requirement to be justifiable.

What does "justifiable" mean?

In order to show a requirement or condition to be justifiable, the employer must satisfy the tribunal that it is relevant to the job for which you have applied and that there is a good reason for it. The tribunal will also need to be satisfied that there is no non-discriminatory way, which it would be reasonable for the employer to adopt, to achieve the same purpose. A further factor which the tribunal will consider is whether the employer has followed the advice contained in any current code of practice under the Race Relations Act. A justification on racial grounds will not do.

Language requirements

You have been turned down for a job because you cannot speak English well enough. In order to decide whether the requirement is justifiable, the tribunal will have regard to the kind of job for which you have applied. If it is a job as a sales representative, receptionist or telephonist or a management or personnel job they are likely to regard the requirement as justifiable. These are jobs which cannot possibly be carried out by a person who cannot speak and understand English. If you wish to become eligible for these jobs then you must learn the language.

On the other hand a language requirement is much less likely to be held to be justifiable if you have applied for a job as a labourer or some other manual job where there is little or no need for you to communicate with other people. For example:

ii   You were born in Pakistan. You have difficulty in speaking and understanding English. You apply for a job operating machines in a factory. The job is one of which you have experience. You

are turned down for the job on the ground tha...
English well enough.

In the above example your claim of indirect discrimina... k
probably succeed. The employer will have great difficulty in satisfy...
the industrial tribunal that a good knowledge of English is necessary
for a job operating machines. It will also be up to the employer to
satisfy the tribunal that the language requirement was not imposed
just to keep out you and other coloured applicants for jobs. If the
employer cannot satisfy the tribunal of this then you will be awarded
compensation.

What if the employer tries to argue that he needs someone who can
at least understand English, because the job involves working with
dangerous machinery and it is essential for employees to be able to read
safety notices. It is unlikely that this defence will succeed, because it
would not be placing an unreasonable strain on the employer's
resources for safety notices to be displayed in languages other than
English or for the employer to take additional steps to bring safety
precautions to the notice of employees.

There is a further point here. You may be able to speak and
understand English well but have difficulty in reading and writing in
English. On the other hand you may be able to read and write English
well, having learned at school, but have difficulty in carrying on a
conversation in English. If you apply for a job which involves talking
to people but not reading or writing, then the employer should rely on
an interview and not expect you to complete a written test. If on the
other hand you apply for a clerical job which does not involve much
speaking to other people then it could be justifiable for the employer to
rely on a written test rather than on an interview.

A requirement to be able to speak and understand English well is not
the only kind of language requirement that could give rise to a claim of
indirect discrimination. For example:

iii   You were born in England and work as a local government
       officer. You apply for a senior post with a local authority in
       Wales. All the people in the area speak English, but the council
       have resolved that only a Welsh speaker will be considered for
       the job. The council are anxious to promote the use of the Welsh
       language. The council will not be able to justify the requirement,

.. to do with your ability to do the job

Some ·

be·
..al **requirements**

There have been cases of employers refusing to consider applicants who live in a particular area. This could be because the employer has previously taken on people from that area who have proved to be trouble makers or it could just be that the area has a bad reputation. If you are a respectable person living in the area and you are turned down for a job because of where you live you will feel annoyed and may wish to consider whether you can bring a claim against the employer. If you can show that the area in which you live contains an unusually high proportion of members of your racial group then your claim will probably succeed. The employer will find it very difficult to satisfy the industrial tribunal that the requirement was justifiable because any sensible employer looks at job applicants as individuals and does not write people off simply because of where they happen to live. However, you will not be awarded compensation if the employer can satisfy the industrial tribunal that it was not his intention simply to exclude the members of your racial group and that he would have refused to consider any applicant from the area, of whatever colour.

It would also be indirect discrimination if the owner of a factory in a mainly white area insisted on employing only people who lived near the factory. The employer could not justify the requirement by showing that the factory was not well served by public transport and that people further away would have had difficulty in getting to work, because many workers have their own form of transport, whether a car or a motorbike or a bicycle.

Educational qualifications

You may be surprised to learn that you could possibly bring a successful claim because an employer has insisted on educational qualifications which you do not have. It is an established and surely a reasonable custom for employers to ask for a minimum number of 'O' or 'A' level passes or for a university degree. If they did not ask applicants for their certificates and degrees en... *ination* jobs have to hold their own examinations and many lack either the resources or the ability to do this. *for many*

There are however two circumstances in which you could *would* grounds for complaint. The first is if the qualifications which the employer is asking for are excessive in relation to the job. For example, an employer would probably find it difficult to justify having insisted on 'O' levels or 'A' levels for an ordinary manual job or a university degree for a routine clerical job.

You could also have a claim for indirect discrimination if an employer refuses to recognise certificates or degrees which you have obtained overseas. For example:

iv   You came to England as a boy having obtained in India the equivalent of three 'A' levels. You apply to a large company for an administrative job and your application is turned down because you do not have any 'A' levels. You will have little difficulty in proving the discriminatory effect of the requirement. The company will have great difficulty in justifying their refusal to take account of overseas qualifications of a similar standard to 'A' levels. However, they will be able to avoid having to pay compensation to you if they can satisfy the tribunal that the requirement was a long standing one and that it had simply never occurred to them that it had a discriminatory effect.

It is not only employers who sometimes insist on educational qualifications. The following example of discrimination by a qualifying body is based on an actual case:

v   You have lived in England for many years but you obtained your degree overseas before you came to England. You wish to enter a profession. In order to do so you must take a course and then sit an examination run by the governing body of the profession. This body allows graduates of British universities to take a one year course but other people, including graduates of foreign universities, must take a two year course. The reason for the requirement is that the two year course would give persons from overseas extra time to become familiar with the British way of life before entering the profession. The requirement has a

Some Comm⋅⋅ ⋅⋅ one which the professional body to be justifiable. Attendance at a British discrimin⋅⋅ ⋅⋅t the only way to acquire a knowledge of the will ⋅way of life.

Experience

If you are looking for work for the first time or are trying to change to a different kind of job, you may find that employers refuse to consider you because you have no experience of doing the kind of work required. This is a requirement which will often be upheld by tribunals, especially where the job is one where experience is important. The employer could argue that it would be unreasonable to expect him to take on people with no experience of the work when there are applicants who have several years' experience. These applicants will not require a lengthy period of training before they can start doing productive work. However, it is possible that if the job is one which can easily be picked up the industrial tribunal would take the view that the employer was being unduly rigid in insisting on seeing only experienced applicants, particularly where the effect would be that an industry in which all the workers are white will remain exclusive to white workers. Furthermore, there are some jobs where academic or technical qualifications are at least as important as experience in the job and it may be unjustifiable for an employer to refuse to consider you if you have such qualifications but no experience in the job.

It is not only when actually applying for jobs that you may face the requirement that you must have previous experience. The following example is based on an actual case:

vi   You are a post graduate of African origin. You obtain a place at a polytechnic for a management studies course. You then apply to the Manpower Services Commission for sponsorship under the "Tops" scheme. Your application is turned down because you have no prior managerial experience. You take your case to an industrial tribunal. It is accepted by the tribunal that the criterion of experience is likely to affect a disproportionately large number of black applicants. However, the Manpower

Services Commission argue that if the requirement were removed the credibility of the scheme would be damaged and people like you would simply be training for unemployment. The tribunal accepts the evidence given on behalf of the Manpower Services Commission and finds the requirement to be justifiable.

Trade Union Membership

An even more common requirement which you will come up against when you are applying for jobs is that you must be a member of a trade union. This requirement has been established in many industries after lengthy disputes and negotiations between employers and trade unions and employers would argue that they could not simply remove the requirement without damaging industrial relations. Most industrial tribunals would probably accept this argument. However, you could find yourself in a vicious circle. For example:

vii   Having completed a training course you apply for a skilled job for which you are qualified. The employer will consider your application only if you are a trade union member. You apply to join the trade union but are told that you will be accepted only if you have already worked in the industry. You are black and virtually all the existing members of the trade union are white. A claim against the trade union could well succeed. If the trade union try to justify their policy you could argue that where a closed shop operates throughout an industry it is unreasonable for the trade union to be unduly strict in their membership requirements. You could go on to argue that it is not a legitimate function of trade unions to raise the wages of their members by artificially keeping down the numbers in the industry, especially where the effect is that the industry remains one exclusively for white workers.

Religion

Religious discrimination as such is not unlawful. If an employer in Great Britain (but not Northern Ireland) is prejudiced against Roman Catholics he can simply refuse to employ them. However, there are some religious requirements which may be indirectly discriminatory in their effect on members of certain racial groups. For example, if an employer requires applicants for a job to certify that they are not Muslims, this requirement is one which would disqualify a comparatively high proportion of Pakistani and probably of African applicants. Even if the employer is willing to accept an instant conversion, it is unlikely that a tribunal would ever accept that a requirement that to be eligible for a job you must change your religion is one with which you "can comply" in any real sense. Indeed in view of a firm ruling by the House of Lords (see the Introduction, Page 6) it would not be open to a tribunal to accept this.

In most circumstances a religious requirement would not be held to be justifiable. For example:

viii   You are a Muslim, born in Pakistan. You apply for a vacancy at a factory but the works manager refuses to consider you for the job because of your religion. He tells you that the last Muslim employed by the company kept taking time off for prayer and accordingly he is not willing to consider any other Muslims. You tell him that you will not need to ask for any time off during normal working hours but this makes no difference. The employer will not be able to justify the requirement. It is reasonable that he should wish to satisfy himself that anyone he takes on will attend for work during usual working hours, but is is not reasonable for him to rule you out because of his experiences with a previous worker of the same religion.

There are a few jobs where it would probably be held to be justifiable for an employer to refuse to consider you and other applicants of your religion. For example, you cannot expect to succeed in a claim of indirect discrimination if you apply for a job as a teacher in an Anglican school or as a journalist on a church newspaper and cannot comply with a requirement that the successful candidate must be a Christian.

Dress and appearance

As mentioned in the Introduction (Page 6), you could have a claim if, as a member of a racial group, you cannot comply with a requirement relating to your dress or appearance. If, however, you succeed in showing that such a requirement is indirectly discriminatory against you as a member of a racial group, there are still two ways in which your claim could fail. First, the employer could show the requirement to be justifiable. For example:

ix   You are a Sikh and your religion requires you not to shave your beard. You apply for a job in a food factory. The employer refuses to consider you for the job because there is a requirement that all employees, of whatever colour, must be clean shaven. This requirement has been imposed for reasons of hygiene and the employer is able to satisfy the industrial tribunal that there is no practicable alternative. Your claim of indirect discrimination fails.

Secondly, your claim may fail because any indirect discrimination against you is authorised by some statutory regulation. For example:

x   You are a young woman of Asian origin and you have to wear trousers in order to conform with the customs of your community. You apply for a job in which a uniform must be worn. The uniform, which does not include trousers, has been prescribed by regulations which have the force of law. You can do nothing about any indirect discrimination which is necessary to comply with the statutory regulations.

Advertisements

There is one final general point which you should bear in mind. If you see an advertisement for a job which you want and the advertisement puts you off applying because it contains some requirement which you cannot comply with, it is possible that an industrial tribunal hearing your complaint of indirect discrimination will find in your favour even if you have not actually applied for the job. You will not be complaining about the advertisement as such but about the employer's recruiting arrangements which have excluded you from consideration for a job which you would have applied for. The advertisement will be relevant only as evidence of these arrangements and of the requirements or condition imposed by the employer.

However, to be on the safe side, where you are interested in a job and find a requirement or condition which you cannot comply with stated in an advertisement or in the application form for the job you should still apply for the job. In your letter you should tell the employer that you cannot comply with the requirement or condition but say that nevertheless you consider that you are suitable for the job and you would like to be considered. If the employer refuses to consider you for the job then you can think about bringing a claim of indirect discrimination.

Summary of Chapter 4

1. You should use the questionnaire procedure in order to establish whether you have been turned down because you cannot comply with a requirement or condition and, if so, what that requirement or condition is.
2. In order to show a requirement or condition to be justifiable an employer must prove that it is relevant to the job and that it is reasonable and that there is no reasonable non-discriminatory alternative. The employer will also be expected to show that he has considered the relevant advice contained in any current Code of Practice under the Act.
3. The main kinds of requirement and condition which may sometimes be held to be indirectly discriminatory are those relating to:
   (a) Ability to speak or write English.
   (b) Place or length of residence.
   (c) Degrees and other educational qualifications.
   (d) Experience of similar work.
   (e) Trade union membership.
   (f) Membership or non-membership of some particular religion.
   (g) Willingness to dress in a particular way or to alter your appearance (by shaving off your beard).

5

What you should do about discrimination

The advice given in this chapter is on the assumption that your complaint is against an employer who has turned you down for a job. Most of it applies also to complaints against trade unions, training bodies, qualifying bodies and employment agencies.

This chapter outlines the various steps which you should take if you believe that there has been racial discrimination against you and you wish to do something about it. There are four points in particular which you should always bear in mind. First of all you should always be willing to consider a fair settlement of your claim, either before or after applying to have your case heard by a tribunal. Secondly, if you do take your case to a tribunal, it is up to you to prove that there has been discrimination against you and you must make sure that your case is properly prepared and presented. Thirdly, there are several places where you may be able to obtain expert advice and assistance, often free of charge, to help you prepare and perhaps present your case. Fourthly, there is a very short time limit within which you must apply to have your case heard by a tribunal.

Time limit

There are several things which you should do or at least consider doing before you apply to have your case heard by a tribunal. However, you must always bear in mind that in order to have your case heard you must make sure that your application is received at the Tribunal Central Office within three months after the act of discrimination which you are complaining about.

You must not wait until the last day or two of the three months before you send off the form. Remember that the form must be actually received at the Tribunal Central Office within the three month period. Send off the form at least a couple of weeks before the end of the period.

From what date do you start counting the three months? Sometimes this will be obvious, if you have applied for a job and been turned down on the same day. In other cases you may not know when the employer decided not to offer you the job or offer you an interview. For example:

i   You apply for a job and attend for an interview. At the interview the employer promises to let you know but you never hear anything from the employer. You ring up three weeks later and are told that somebody else has been given the job. To be on the safe side you should assume that the three months starts to run from the date of your interview.

If you apply for a job and are not offered an interview then, again to be on the safe side, you should assume that the three months starts from the date when your application would have been received by the employer.

The time limit of three months is absolutely vital. If your application is not received in time, the tribunal will almost certainly refuse to hear your case, even if you have absolutely conclusive evidence of racial discrimination. The tribunal has the power to extend the three months period but the power is exercised only very rarely and only when there is a very good reason for the delay. It is not a good reason to say that you simply forgot to send the application form in or did not realise how quickly time was slipping past.

If it has been impossible for you to send the form in before the three months are up, you must do so at the earliest possible moment, to have the best chance of obtaining an extension.

Picking up the forms

Even though you may not be sending the application form to the Tribunal Office for a couple of months or so, you should pick the form up immediately. The form is headed "Originating Application To An Industrial Tribunal" and is known as a Form IT 1. You may obtain the form free of charge from your local jobcentre, an employment office or an employment benefit office. If you do not know the address of the nearest office look in the telephone directory under "Employment, department of" or "Employment Service Division of the Manpower Services Commission".

As well as two copies of the originating application form IT 1 you will also require several other documents which will all be supplied free of charge. These are the booklet ITL 1 which explains about industrial tribunal procedure, a Guide to the Race Relations Act and two copies of a booklet which is numbered RR 65. This booklet RR 65 is the one which you will use for the questions procedure, mentioned below. Remember to ask for all these forms. If you have any difficulty your local Community Relations Officer may well have sets of all the forms, including the IT 1.

Help with your case

Most people who have successfully taken their case to a tribunal have had a lawyer or some other expert to represent them at the hearing. A hearing by an industrial tribunal is meant to be informal so that workers and employers can feel at home and present their own cases. The chairman is there to help you with the law and the procedure and the other two members of the tribunal are there for their practical knowledge of what actually happens in industry. Even so, it can be difficult to do justice to your case if you are having to explain your case and question all the witnesses as well as give your own evidence.

It may not be possible for you to obtain free representation at the hearing of your case. However, there are several ways in which you may be able to obtain free help and advice with the preparation of your case. You should always try to obtain this help and advice right away and not wait until you have applied to have your case heard by a tribunal.

Where should you go for expert advice? One obvious place is the Commission for Racial Equality. One of their main functions is to help people like you. The addresses and telephone numbers of the regional offices of the Commission are set out in the appendix at the end of this book. You should telephone your nearest office at the earliest opportunity to arrange to see a complaints officer to discuss your case.

If your case raises some important point of principle or there is some other good reason why you should be represented at the hearing then the Commission may be willing to pay for a solicitor or barrister to represent you or send along one of its own complaints officers to represent you. Even if this is not possible (because the Commission has limited funds), the Commission will almost certainly give you advice about your case. You will find it invaluable to discuss your case in detail with someone who is objective and knows a good deal about racial discrimination law.

Another way to obtain free advice is to go to a solicitor who is prepared to give advice under what is known as the "green form" scheme. This scheme does not cover the cost of having a solicitor actually appearing for you at the hearing. Unfortunately legal aid is not available for representation at industrial tribunal hearings. However, under this scheme you can go along to a solicitor and discuss your case and obtain advice and all this may be free of charge. You should start off by telling the solicitor that you would like to consider having advice under the "green form" scheme and give him details of your income, savings and dependants. The solicitor will then either tell you that he can discuss your case (for a limited period) and give you advice free of charge or tell you how much you will have to pay if you decide to stay to discuss your case. You can find out more about the scheme and find out the names and addresses of solicitors who will see you under the scheme by going along to your local Citizens Advice Bureau.

There are other ways in which you may be able to obtain free advice and perhaps even free representation at the hearing. One is by approaching a law centre, if you live near one. Another is by asking your trade union for help, if you belong to one. The union may be willing to pay for you to see a local solicitor or it may have its own legal officer who can advise you and perhaps even represent you at the hearing. Remember that if you wish to have someone to present your case for you at the tribunal hearing your representative does not have to be a lawyer. It could be an official from your trade union for instance.

If you do not belong to a union and you do not live near one of the regional offices of the Commission for Racial Equality or near a law centre and feel nervous (although you need not do so) about approaching a solicitor then you could telephone or call to see your local Community Relations Officer, who will usually be willing to suggest where you should turn for advice. Indeed the CRO may be prepared to deal with your case personally and even to represent you at the hearing.

When you go to see anyone to discuss your case, you should take with you the application form IT 1 and the questions booklet and the other documents which you have picked up. You should also take any documents which you have concerning your case, like the advertisement for the job which you applied for, a copy of your application for the job (if you have kept a copy) and any letter which you have received from the employer.

Having turned up with your documents, what should you discuss and what will you need to ask advice about? Obviously you will wish to discuss whether, on the facts as you know them, there has been unlawful discrimination against you and how you can go about proving your case. You should also ask for advice about using the questions procedure and completing the application form IT 1. You should also discuss whether an attempt should be made to negotiate a settlement of your claim without a tribunal hearing.

Trying to settle your case

Most of the people who take their claims all the way to a tribunal hearing lose their cases, but many cases are settled before they reach that stage. There are two reasons why you should never allow anger about the way in which you have been treated to stand in the way of a fair settlement of your case.

First of all, if you have been turned down for a job and are still out of work, then presumably your main aim will be to obtain a job. Money to compensate you for having been turned down cannot be a satisfactory substitute. However, even if you take your case to a tribunal hearing and win, the tribunal cannot make the employer offer you a job. They can make a recommendation to that effect, but all that they can do if the employer unreasonably fails to comply with the recommendation is award you extra compensation. You will still be out of work. If you want to persuade the employer to reconsider the decision not to employ you and to offer you a job, you probably have a better chance of doing so at an early stage rather than when the employer is resentful because of the accusations made against him at the hearing and the finding of discrimination made by the tribunal.

Secondly, even if the employer remains unwilling to offer you a job, he may be willing to offer a reasonable amount of compensation in order to avoid the inconvenience, expense and publicity of a hearing and the risk of a decision against him by the tribunal. If you accept a fair offer of compensation before the hearing then you will save yourself the possible anxiety and stress of the hearing, you will not have to wait as long for your money and you will avoid the risk of losing your case and receiving nothing at all. On the other hand, most employers would fight a claim which they saw as a pure "try-on".

How should you do about trying to settle your case? It may be worthwhile making an immediate approach to the employer, either personally or through your solicitor or union, the Commission for Racial Equality or a CRO. If the decision to discriminate against you was not made at the highest level in the company, then you should make an approach to a more senior member of the company, such as the chairman or managing director. It may turn out that the discrimination against you was unauthorised and that the chairman or managing director, when he finds out about it, is anxious to put matters right, by offering you either a job or a fair amount by way of compensation.

Even after you have started proceedings there will still be a possibility of reaching agreement with the employer. A conciliation officer of ACAS will receive a copy of the application form which you send to the tribunal office. He is under a duty to try to promote a settlement of your claim if he thinks that there is a reasonable prospect of success or if both you and the employer wish him to. If your case does go to a hearing, then nothing you have said to the conciliation officer can be used in evidence against you without your consent. Equally, you cannot use against the employer any statement made to you by the conciliation officer.

The questions procedure

Examples have been given in Chapters 3 and 4 of the ways in which the questions procedure which is available under the Act can be useful in helping you to decide whether or not to take your case to a tribunal. When you called at the jobcentre, employment office or unemployment benefit office for the application form IT 1 you will also have asked for two copies of the booklet containing the questions. There are notes in the booklet containing guidance on the way in which you should prepare the questionnaire. You should read these notes carefully. In addition, as already mentioned in this chapter, you should try to obtain expert help on filling in the questionnaire so that you can choose the questions which are appropriate to your own case.

At the top of the questionnaire you have to give the name and address of the employer and then in question one you state your own name and address. Question 2 should contain a very brief statement of the facts which you are complaining about. For example:

ii   You are black. You apply for a job and are interviewed by a personnel manager. You suspect, because of his aggressive manner and the questions which he asks you, that he is prejudiced against you. You subsequently receive a letter from him turning you down for the job. All that you need to say as question 2 on the questionnaire is something like this:
"On (date) I applied to (name of employer) for a job as a (kind of job). On (date) I was interviewed by (the name of the personnel officer), the personnel officer. On (date) I received a letter from (name of personnel officer) stating that my application for the job had been unsuccessful."

Leave out any dates or names if you are not sure of them. It is not necessary for you to go into great detail. For example you should not say what the personnel officer said to you and what you said to him and you do not need to say why you think he seemed to be prejudiced against you.

In question 3 you can if you wish state why you believe that you may have been treated unlawfully. You do not have to answer this question at all. You could just cross out the word "because".

You should not alter questions 4 and 5 on the form. Question 4 asks whether the employer agrees with your statement of what happened to you and, if not, in what respects he disagrees. Question 5 asks why you were treated in this way (ie why you were turned down for the job), whether your treatment was affected by any racial ground and whether the employer accepts that you were treated unlawfully (and if not, why not). These are key questions. There is then a space for you to ask additional questions. Note 13 with the form suggests a question which you could ask if you think that there may have been indirect discrimination against you and note 14 suggests a question which is relevant if you suspect victimisation.

If you suspect direct discrimination against you, you should ask in this space for details of the colour, nationality and ethnic or national origin of the successful candidate and also details of his or her qualifications and experience. If you were refused an interview for the job then you will need to ask for similar details about all the applicants who were offered an interview.

If, when you asked about the job, you were told that the vacancy had already been filled, then you will need to ask for the exact date and time when the successful applicant was offered the job.

Another question which is often asked is how many black or brown employees the employer has. However the answer to this question is not likely to help your case and may indeed be helpful to the employer. If the employer replies that he has no black or brown employees, this is not evidence of discrimination because there could be a perfectly good reason. Perhaps no black or brown person has ever before applied for a job with the employer. If on the other hand the employer has a number of black or brown employees then he could argue at the hearing that this is evidence that he is not prejudiced. As we shall see later in this chapter (example vii), when considering the hearing itself, there are a number of possible answers to this argument, but it is more difficult for you to give those answers if by asking the question you have shown that you regard the matter as relevant.

In question 7 on the form you should indicate whether you want the reply to the questions to be sent to your own address or some other address. If, for example, you have a solicitor advising you, you may wish to give the solicitor's address as that to which the reply must be sent.

Having completed both copies of the form you should keep one and send the other to the employer. Usually the address of the employer to which you should send the form will be the office, shop or factory at which you applied for the job. However, if the employer is a limited company the form should be sent to the registered office of the company. You may have correspondence from the company showing the address of the registered office. If not, you will be able to obtain the information by asking at the reference department of your public library. You should send the form by recorded delivery post.

You can send the questions to the employer either before you have applied to have your case heard by a tribunal or within 21 days after your application has been received at the Tribunal Office. However, it is preferable to send the form to the employer within a week or so after the discrimination which you are complaining about, because the reply to the form may help you decide whether or not to take your case to a tribunal.

Applying to have your case heard

You should complete two copies of the form IT 1. As already mentioned, you should try to obtain expert help with the form. If you have used the questions procedure, then you will be able to copy some of the details from the questions form. Altogether there are fourteen questions on the form IT 1, but several of these questions are not relevant when you are complaining about discrimination against you as an applicant for a job.

In answer to question 1, you have to say what kind of case it is that you wish the tribunal to hear. The industrial tribunals do not only deal with racial discrimination cases. They also hear many other cases, including claims of unfair dismissal. If you wish to complain about direct or indirect racial discrimination then simply write "racial discrimination". If you are complaining about victimisation then you should put "victimisation (under the Race Relations Act)". If you think that there could have been either racial discrimination or sex discrimination against you then you should put "racial discrimination and sex discrimination".

Questions 2 and 3 are fairly straightforward. Question 2 requires your own full name and address, telephone number and date of birth. In reply to question 3 you have to state the name, address and telephone number of any representative, such as a solicitor, who has agreed to act for you. Any future communications will be sent to that representative and you and your representative must make sure that details of any communications are passed on to you.

Question 4 requires you to state the name, address and telephone number of the person whom you wish to complain about. If you are complaining about having been turned down for a job then this person will be the employer. If the employer is a company and you do not know the registered office of the company you can find this out by going to the reference department of your public library. If there is no time for this, because the three months time limit has nearly expired, then you should put the address to which you applied for the job.

The person you are complaining about is known as the respondent and you will be known as the applicant. If you were turned down for the job by someone who works for the employer, like a personnel officer, you should consider putting that person down as an extra respondent, in case the employer manages to establish that the discrimination against you was unauthorised and that all reasonable practicable steps had been taken by the employer to prevent the discrimination. If you do not know the name and address of the person who turned you down then you will have to ask the employer. If you are anywhere near the three months deadline do not delay sending off the form until you have the information. Send it off showing the employer as the respondent.

In the second part of question 4 you have to state the respondent's relationship to you for the purpose of the application. This will be "employer" (or, strictly speaking, "prospective employer").

Of course if you are not complaining about discrimination by an employer to whom you applied for a job but discrimination by some other body, such as a trade union, then you would give the name and address of the trade union in the first part of question 4. In the second part you would state "trade union" (if it is a union that you are complaining about).

The next question, number 5, asks where the act complained about took place. This will be the address of the office, factory or shop to which you applied for the job or where you were interviewed.

Then in question 6 you should state the kind of job which you applied for. The next four questions are not relevant when you are complaining about discrimination against you as an applicant for a job.

In question 11 you have to state the date on which the act you are complaining about took place or first came to your knowledge. You should put the date on which you were informed your application for the job was unsuccessful. If you were never told the result of your application you should put "on or after (the date of your last communication from the employer or, if there was never any communication, the date of your application for the job)".

In question 12 you are required to state the grounds of your application. You should give a short statement of the facts similar to that suggested for question 2 of the questions form. You should then say something like "I believe that I was refused the job on racial grounds". You may state very briefly the reason for this belief (for example, that you were told by the employer that the vacancy had been filled when in fact it had not), but this is not essential and certainly you should not put down all your evidence and full details of all the relevant conversations.

You should ignore questions 13 and 14, which are relevant only if you have been dismissed. You should then sign and date the form.

You should keep one copy of the form and send the other to the Central Office of the industrial tribunals. The address and telephone number are given near the top of Page 1 of the form.

You should not wait until the day before the three months are up before you send off the form. Send the form at least a couple of weeks before the end of the three months. If you have heard nothing within a week or so there will still be time for you to telephone the Tribunal Office to find out if the application has been received and send in a fresh application if the first one has gone astray. Find the telephone number by looking at Page 1 of the copy of the application form which you have kept.

You should also send the Tribunal Office a copy of your questionnaire and any reply, either now or at least before the hearing.

71

Further particulars

When your application is received at the Tribunal Central Office, two things will happen. A written acknowledgment will be sent to you and you will be told which tribunal regional office you should send future correspondence to. The tribunal office will also send a copy of your application to the respondent, who will have fourteen days to give notice of appearance. In this document, the respondent must state whether or not he will be contesting your claim and, if he is contesting it, on what grounds.

It is possible that your application form IT 1 does not contain enough information to enable the respondent to decide whether or not to contest your claim. For example:

iii   You telephone about a job which has been advertised. The receptionist can tell from your name and your accent that you are of Asian origin. She tells you that the vacancy has been filled. Later that day a white friend of yours telephones about the same job and is offered an interview. You send off your form IT 1 stating the date on which you applied for the job and the fact that your application was turned down. However, you do not state that your application was made by telephone. When they receive the application the employers make enquiries but nobody admits to having spoken to you. They do not know whether you applied in writing or turned up at the office or spoke to the personnel manager or spoke to somebody else. Accordingly they write to you asking for further particulars of your application, namely the way in which you applied for the job and the name of the person who refused your application. You should supply these particulars, stating that you applied for the job by telephone and spoke to the receptionist who told you that the vacancy had been filled. If you refuse to give the information then the employers can ask the tribunal to make an order requiring you to do so.

Similarly, you may require further particulars of information given by the employers, either in the rely to the questionnaire or in the notice of appearance. In the above example, if the employers simply deny that there was any discrimination against you, you will not know whether they are saying that you were never told that the vacancy had been filled or whether they are saying that the vacancy had in fact been filled when you telephoned. You are entitled to ask for these particulars. You should do so by writing to the employers asking for the information and specifying a time (not unreasonably short) within which the information is to be given. You should keep a copy of your letter. If the particulars requested are not given by the employers within the stated time you should write to the tribunal office, with a copy of the letter which you sent to the employers, asking for an order for the employers to give the particulars requested.

Pre-hearing assessment

The tribunal may decide to hold a pre-hearing assessment to consider the content of either your originating application to the tribunal or the respondent's notice of appearance. The tribunal may decide to do this either of its own accord or at the request of either party.

No evidence is given at the pre-hearing assessment and no witnesses need attend. The purpose of the assessment is to let you know if your case is clearly a hopeless one. The tribunal cannot stop you carrying on and taking your case to a full hearing but if you do you will run the risk of being ordered to pay the respondent's costs. For example:

iv   You have only recently come to live in England. You can write English well but have not yet learned to speak the language. You apply for a job as a sales representative and are offered an interview. You are turned down for the job and you send off an originating application complaining of racial discrimination. In their notice of appearance the employers state that they turned you down for the job because at the interview they simply could not understand a word that you were saying. You could neither speak English nor understand spoken English. The tribunal decide to hold a pre-hearing assessment and you are invited to attend (together with your representative if you have one). When you do attend it is obvious that the employers are right in saying that you cannot speak English. You are warned that your case does not appear to have any substance and that if you insist on going to a full hearing and losing then you will probably be ordered to pay the employers' costs.

73

The pre-hearing assessment can work both ways. It could be the employer who is warned that he is at risk of having to pay your costs if he persists with a hopeless defence. For example:

v Your application for a job is turned down and you send an originating application to the Tribunal Office. In their notice of appearance the employers admit that they turned down your application on racial grounds but state that they had to do so in order to avoid unrest amongst their existing employees. The tribunal decide to hold a pre-hearing assessment. The employers are invited to attend and are told that their defence is a hopeless one, because fear of upsetting other employees is not a legitimate reason for discrimination. They are warned that if they insist on contesting your claim and they lose then they will probably be ordered to pay all your costs.

If you are going to be represented at the hearing and you are invited to attend a pre-hearing assessment, ask your representative to go with you.

Documents

Sometimes, in order to prove your case, you may need to refer to documents which are in the employer's possession. If the employer has turned you down after an interview, then the relevant documents will include the notes made by the employer during your interview and the notes made during the interview of the successful applicant. If you have made a written application for the job but been refused an interview then the relevant documents will include your application and also the applications received from all the people who were offered interviews. You can insist on the employer producing any relevant documents in his possession.

You should write in good time to the employer telling him which documents you wish him to produce at the hearing and asking him to make the documents available to you for inspection beforehand or, preferably, to send copies of the documents to you. In your letter you should specify the period (not unreasonably short) within which the employer should make the documents available to you or supply copies of them. You should keep a copy of your letter.

If the employer refuses to produce the documents within the period specified or ignores your letter you should write to the tribunal office (at the address given to you). You should enclose a copy of the letter which you sent to the respondent (the employer) and ask for an order for the respondent to make the documents available for inspection and to produce the documents at the hearing.

The tribunal has the power to order the respondent to produce even confidential documents. There is a rule of law (as mentioned in the Introduction) that the tribunal must make the order for production of the documents when this is necessary to enable you to prove your case or otherwise to do justice between you and the respondent. If you do receive copies of confidential documents you must of course use them only for the purposes of your own case at the tribunal hearing and not for any ulterior purpose.

You should also ask the respondent well in advance for details of any documents which he will be relying on at the hearing. Industrial tribunals do not approve of either party keeping important documents back so as to spring them on the other party at the hearing. If the respondent will be relying on some document which you do not have a copy of then you should ask him to produce the document for inspection by you or let you have a copy.

The rule about relevant documents being produced works both ways. If the respondent wishes to rely on some document which you have then you must produce the document at the hearing and also make the document available to the respondent for inspection beforehand. This could happen, if, for instance, the respondent wishes to refer to the letter sent to you turning down your application and can no longer find a copy of that letter.

You should in any event take along to the hearing all the documents in your possession which could be relevant. One thing which the tribunal will want to know something about, if your claim is successful, is what has happened to you since you were turned down for the job. Have you been successful in obtaining another job and if so at what wage? You should take these details along with you together with any relevant documents, such as wage slips.

Another document which will often be relevant, especially when you are complaining about indirect discrimination, is any newspaper advertisement which you read before you applied for the job and you should take the advertisement with you to the hearing. If when you applied for the job a special application form was provided and if there are also accompanying notes about the job and details of conditions of employment all these documents will be relevant.

Witnesses

You may well be the only person giving evidence in support of your case. If, for example, your case is based on what was said to you at an interview, then you are probably the only person apart from the employer or his staff to have been present at the interview.

Sometimes, however, you will wish to call another witness as well. For example, if you have applied for a job and been told that the job has been filled you may have arranged for a white friend to apply for the same job. If that friend was then offered an interview you will wish to call your friend to give evidence on your behalf. Or perhaps you have applied for a job through a jobcentre and the interviewer at the jobcentre spoke to the employer on your behalf and was told by the employer that he was not willing to see you because of your colour.

If you have a witness to call in support of your case then you should give the name and address of the witness to your solicitor or whoever is handling the case on your behalf and arrange for him or her to see the witness as soon as possible. If you are handling your own case then you should obtain a full written statement from the witness and not simply turn up at the hearing without knowing exactly what the witness will be saying. You should also consider writing to the local tribunal office with the name and address of the witness and asking for an order for the witness to attend the hearing. This may be necessary either because you feel that the witness may let you down or because the witness will have difficulty in getting time off work unless he or she has been formally required to attend.

It is essential that any witness whose evidence you need should attend the hearing and not just give you a written statement. On the other hand it is not usually a good idea to insist on the attendance of a witness who could be hostile to you.

If your witness is worried that he or she may get into trouble for giving evidence on your behalf you must point out that victimisation of a person for giving evidence in good faith in a racial discrimination case is against the law. If the witness is worried about losing money as a result of attending the hearing, you should point out that after the hearing he or she will be able to claim travelling expenses and allowances for subsistence and loss of earnings.

Written statement

You will be given at least fourteen days notice of the date of the hearing of your case. The tribunal rules of procedure contain a provision under which you may submit written representations to the tribunal at least seven days before the hearing. A copy of the statement must be sent to the respondent at the same time.

This procedure can be useful if you have had advice about your case but will be conducting your own case at the tribunal hearing. Your adviser can help you prepare, or can prepare for you, a statement setting out a summary of your case and any legal arguments which are relevant and then at the hearing you will be able to concentrate on making sure that all the relevant facts are placed before the tribunal.

Postponements and withdrawals

If for any reason you cannot attend the hearing on the date which has been fixed then you must let both the tribunal and the respondent know right away. You should telephone them both immediately and also write by first class post on the same day explaining exactly why you cannot attend. If you know a couple of weeks before the hearing date that you will not be able to attend but leave it until the day before the hearing before you let anyone know then the tribunal will probably order you to pay the unnecessary costs which the respondent has incurred.

Similarly, if you decide to drop your case, you must let the tribunal and respondent know immediately. If you do nothing at all and simply fail to turn up at the tribunal hearing then the respondent will certainly ask the tribunal to make an order that you should pay the costs incurred by the respondent in having to turn up with his witnesses and legal adviser.

The hearing itself

If a lawyer or a complaints officer or somebody else is representing you at the hearing then all you will have to do is to answer the questions put to you. You should answer the questions honestly and carefully, using your own words. Whenever you do not understand a question then you should ask for the question to be explained or repeated. Above all, do not be aggressive or obstructive when answering questions put to you by the employer's solicitor or barrister or by the members of the tribunal.

If you are handling your own case then you will usually find it helpful to write down beforehand what you want to say to the tribunal and what you want to ask the employer and his witnesses. On the other hand you must not just read out what you have prepared without listening to the evidence which other people are giving. You should regard the notes which you have made beforehand as a way of getting the facts and arguments clearly in your mind rather than as a speech and a series of questions to be read out.

Before giving your evidence, you should explain briefly to the tribunal the kind of discrimination that you are complaining about and why you contend that discrimination occurred. You should refer briefly to the witnesses and documents you will be relying on. You should also say what remedy you are seeking if your claim is successful. Do you wish the tribunal to make a recommendation that the respondent should offer you a job when another suitable vacancy arises? Or are you so upset by the discrimination against you that you no longer wish to work for the respondent and are asking only for compensation? If the discrimination against you caused you great distress or embarrassment you should mention this, because the tribunal has the power, if your claim is successful, to award compensation for the injury to your feelings. It may be unnecessary for you to make this opening statement if you have sent a written statement to the tribunal and the respondent at least seven days before the hearing.

After you have made your opening statement you will then give evidence. This can be a difficult part of the case, because if you had a representative at the hearing there would be two of you involved, the representative asking questions and you answering them. If you are presenting your own case then it is up to you to state the facts which are within your personal knowledge and to remember to include all the relevant facts. After you have stated the facts you will be questioned by the respondent or his representative. The members of the tribunal will also probably then ask you questions.

After you have been questioned by the respondent's representative you will have the chance to clear up any points arising from this questioning. You should ask the tribunal chairman to be allowed to make a note of any such points as they arise in case you forget them later. For example:

vi You are black. You are complaining about having been turned down for a managerial post in favour of a less qualified white applicant. At the hearing, when the respondent's lawyer is questioning you, he asks you if you accept that the successful white applicant has had more experience in the industry than you have. You accept this. You wish to amplify the answer but the lawyer moves quickly on to the next question. When you come back to this point, at the end of the cross-examination, you tell the tribunal members that the successful applicant has had only slightly more experience than you, that most of this experience was at a lower level whilst yours has been mostly managerial experience and that your technical and academic qualifications are very much superior.

Once your own evidence has been completed, you will then call any witnesses whom you have brought along with you. You must let each witness tell his or her own story in his or her own words and not try to put words into the mouth of the witness. For example if you are asking a witness about a conversation between the witness and the respondent you must not begin a question with the words "did the respondent say to you that ...". Instead you must ask: "What did the respondent say to you?" When one of your witnesses has been cross-examined you will have the opportunity to ask further questions dealing with any points raised in the cross-examination. You must remember to refer to any relevant documents at the appropriate time. Sometimes it will be necessary for you to refer to a document in your evidence and also to ask one of the respondent's witnesses about the same document.

When your own evidence and that of your witnesses has been heard, it will be the turn of the respondent and his witnesses. When you are questioning the respondent's witnesses you must not shout or bluster and you must not expect to be able to trick the witnesses into damaging admissions. You should listen carefully to the evidence given by the respondent's witnesses and take notes of the parts which you do not agree with. You should also make a note of any important facts which a witness has left out of his or her evidence. You should then ask the witness to reconsider the statements which you believe to be false or mistaken. You should also put to the witness the important facts which have been omitted and ask whether he or she agrees those facts. You should also ask the witness to read out any document, including the replies to the questionnaire, which conflicts with the witness's evidence.

After all the evidence has been heard you will have the chance to make a final statement to the tribunal. You should not simply repeat what you said at the start of the case. You should refer to any important facts which are favourable to your case and which have come out during the evidence and you should also try to place in context any evidence which appears to be unfavourable to your case. For example:

vii   The respondent's witnesses have pointed out in evidence that the respondent employs a number of black and brown workers. You point out in your closing speech that this is not reliable evidence that the respondent has not discriminated against you. The job for which you applied was a managerial post and it appears from the evidence that all the black and brown workers employed by the respondent are in manual jobs. One common form of racial prejudice is to regard a black or brown applicant as suitable for certain jobs but unsuitable for more senior posts. Furthermore, it is possible that dissatisfaction with some of the black and brown workers employed by the respondent has caused the respondent to turn down your application. It is not legitimate for an employer to turn down a job application on the basis of past experience with workers of the same colour as the applicant.

Moreover the person who took on these black and brown workers may not be the same as the person who turned down your application.

Compensation, etc.

If you win your case the tribunal will make a declaration that the respondent has discriminated unlawfully against you. They may also recommend that the respondent should offer you a job, either now or when the next vacancy arises. Finally, they will also order the respondent to pay compensation to you, unless your complaint is about indirect discrimination and the respondent has proved that the requirement or condition complained of was not racially motivated.

You will already, in presenting your case, have told the tribunal whether or not you wish them to recommend that the employer should offer you a job. You should also have given them the evidence which they need in order to decide on the amount of compensation, together with any documents in support. The tribunal will wish to know the wage which went with the job for which you were turned down by the respondent; whether you have obtained another job and if so when and at what wage; if you have not yet obtained work, what efforts you have made and what the prospects are. They will also wish to know whether you were upset or embarrassed by the discrimination against you so that they can decide how much to award you for the injury to your feelings.

Unless your case is exceptional, the amount of compensation likely to be awarded to you will be in the hundreds of pounds (or sometimes even less), rather than the thousands of pounds. You are being compensated not for the loss of a job but for the loss of opportunity of being fairly considered for the job. It may be difficult to say whether you would have been offered the job even if you had been fairly considered for it and, if so, for how long you would have kept the job.

Costs

If you lose, the respondent's representative may ask the tribunal to make an order for you to pay the respondent's costs, on the ground that you acted unreasonably in taking your case to a tribunal hearing. You or your representative may make a similar application against the respondent, if you win and if the respondent has acted unreasonably in defending your case. The tribunal are likely to make an order for costs against any party who has been unsuccessful and who has insisted on pressing on with his or her claim or defence in spite of being warned at a pre-hearing assessment that he or she has a hopeless case or defence.

Expenses

After the hearing and before you and your witnesses leave the tribunal building you should all see the tribunal clerk (he or she may approach you) about applying for travelling expenses and subsistence and loss of earnings allowances.

The tribunal decision

The tribunal may give its decision at the end of the hearing but in some cases the decision is given later. Even if the decision is given at the hearing, you will later on receive a document setting out the decision and the reasons for it.

Appeals

If the tribunal decision goes against you you may appeal on a point of law only to the Employment Appeal Tribunal. The respondent has a similar right of appeal. The appeal must be lodged within forty two days after the date stamped on the tribunal decision letter. You should always take legal advice before lodging an appeal. You can apply for legal aid in order to be legally represented at the appeal.

Summary of Chapter 5

1. Always remember that to have your case heard by a tribunal your completed originating application form IT 1 must be received at the Tribunal Central Office within three months after the act of discrimination complained of.

2. Before sending off the originating application you should *if possible*:
   (a) Seek legal advice, which will often be free, eg. from the Commission for Racial Equality, a solicitor or your trade union or local Community Relations Officer.
   (b) Consider approaching the employer to try to settle your claim.
   (c) Use the questions procedure to try to obtain more information.
3. After sending off the application and without any delay you should start preparing your case and if necessary apply to the tribunal office dealing with your case for an order for further particulars of the respondent's case or an order for the respondent to produce relevant documents or a witness order.
4. You should consider discussing your case with an ACAS conciliation officer to see if a settlement can be achieved.
5. If invited to attend a pre-hearing assessment you should do so (with your adviser or representative if you have one) and consider carefully any advice which you are given.
6. You may send a written statement, outlining what you are complaining about and what you are asking the tribunal for, at least seven days before the tribunal hearing (with a copy to the respondent).
7. At the hearing, you want to make sure that the tribunal know what you are complaining about and what remedy you are asking for. You also want to make sure that they have heard evidence from you and your witnesses about all the facts which you think are relevant and that you have contradicted any evidence given by the respondent's witnesses which you do not agree with.
8. If you wish to appeal against the tribunal decision you must do so within forty two days after the date stamped on the tribunal decision letter.

Part II

Discrimination at work

The most common complaint of racial discrimination at work is that the employer has discriminated in deciding who should be promoted or trained for promotion. If your complaint is of this kind you should turn to Chapter 6. This chapter describes ways in which you may be able to recognise and prove direct discrimination against you when you are denied promotion or training. It also gives some examples of indirect discrimination in the choice of employees for promotion or training. First of all, however, it explains that there are a few cases where employers are allowed to discriminate in these matters.

Chapter 7 then deals with other forms of discrimination at work. Your employer must not racially discriminate against you in fixing your wage or your fringe benefits or in deciding what work you should do and under what conditions you should do it. The employer may also be held responsible if your superior at work, such as the head of your department or foreman or supervisor, discriminates against you in making things difficult or unpleasant for you. You may also have a claim if you are punished or dismissed in a way that amounts to racial discrimination.

Many of the exceptions considered in Chapter 2 could in theory apply to discrimination against you as an existing employee as well as discrimination against you as a job applicant, but few of them are likely to occur in practice.

Chapter 8 contains some practical tips for you if you feel that you have been a victim of discrimination at work.

6

Discrimination in promotion and training

The general principle is that employers must not discriminate in deciding which of their employees should be promoted. It does not matter whether you have made a formal application for promotion or whether the employer is simply considering which employees should be offered promotion. Quite often, in order to become qualified for promotion, you need to undergo some sort of training. Again the general rule is that employers must not discriminate in deciding which of their employees should be offered training. The same rule applies when employers are dealing with a request for a transfer to a different kind of work or a different establishment or when they are considering offering a transfer to an employee or asking an employee to take a transfer.

Sometimes, especially if you are working in a professional firm, promotion will mean not being offered a more senior employment but being offered a partnership in the firm. As long as there are at least six partners in the firm, you will have a claim against the firm if they discriminate in failing to offer you promotion. For example:

i   You are an architect of Indian origin employed by a large firm with more than five partners. The partners are considering offering a partnership either to you or to a white colleague, whose experience and paper qualifications are not as good as yours. They decide to offer the partnership to your colleague because the position as a partner would involve dealing with an important customer of the firm who is strongly prejudiced against coloured people. This discrimination against you is unlawful and you could claim compensation.

When is discrimination permitted?

There are very few exceptions to the rule that your employer must not discriminate in deciding whether to offer you promotion, training or a transfer. The only kind of job that falls almost completely outside the Race Relations Act (but not quite – there must be no victimisation and no discrimination against contract workers) is one in a private household. For example:

ii   You are an assistant gardener, working in the large grounds of a private house. When the head gardener leaves your employer refuses to promote you and admits to you that this is because of your colour. This open racial discrimination against you is lawful.

If you are working in the civil service, you may find that you are not eligible for certain posts or transfers to certain departments, because of your place of birth or nationality or that of one of your parents or more remote ancestors. You may very occasionally face lawful discrimination of this kind even if you work for a private company. For example:

iii   You came to Britain as a refugee from Eastern Europe and were naturalised long ago. You work for a firm which has an important defence contract with the British government. You are seeking promotion but the job which you are after would involve a transfer to a department doing top secret work on the defence contract. A government minister has certified that only employees born in Great Britain must be allowed to work in that department. You have no claim under the Race Relations Act.

If the promotion which you are after would involve some sort of social or personnel work, it is possible that an employer may be permitted to reserve the job for members of a particular ethnic group under the genuine occupational qualification exception. For example:

iv   You work as a junior social worker for a local authority. A more senior post becomes vacant, but the job involves working with refugees who have settled in the town. You speak the language of these refugees but your employer refuses to give you the job and brings in an outsider who is from the same country as the refugees. Even if you are better qualified than the person given the job, it is possible that any complaint of discrimination you may bring against the local authority would be dismissed. The local authority would have to satisfy the industrial tribunal that it was reasonable under the circumstances for the job to be reserved for a person of the same national origin as the refugees.

All the above exceptions are of limited importance. They affect mainly people working for private households, a minority of civil servants and some social workers and personnel and probation officers.

Positive discrimination

If positive or reverse discrimination, sometimes known as affirmative action, were permitted this could affect almost any kind of job. The general rule is that positive discrimination is not permitted. Racial discrimination is unlawful, whether it is practised against or in favour of a member of an ethnic minority. For example:

v   You are a white local government officer. You apply for promotion to a more senior post in your department. A black colleague also applies but he has less experience and is less qualified than you. However, he is offered the post. You are told that members of ethnic minority groups are underrepresented in senior posts and that the policy of the council is to discriminate in favour of employees from these groups who are seeking promotion. The council regards this as an equitable policy, because many of the employees being offered promotion in this way will have been denied equal opportunities in the past, and it will also assist council officers in their dealings with the community if a fair racial balance can be achieved. The discrimination against you, however benevolent the motive, is unlawful.

However, although there must be no discrimination in the choice between you and some other candidate for *promotion*, it is sometimes permissible for the employer to discriminate in deciding who should be offered the *training* which may lead to promotion. For example:

vi   You are a white assistant at a department store. A substantial proportion of the staff of the store and an even larger proportion of the people living in the area from which the store recruits its staff are of West Indian origin. Not one of the department heads is West Indian. You and a West Indian colleague apply for a place on a management training course run by the store group. The course is designed for potential heads of department and anybody who goes on the course is likely to become better qualified for promotion than his or her colleagues. Your West Indian colleague is given a place on the course because of her colour. The store can justify this discrimination and defeat a claim by you on either of two grounds. They can point to the disparity between the proportion of department heads who are West Indian and the proportion of the staff as a whole who are West Indian. They can also point to the even greater disparity between the proportion of department heads who are West Indian and the proportion of the people living in the recruitment area who are West Indian. As long as this disparity can be shown to exist either at the time of the appointment or at any time within the previous twelve months the discrimination against you and in favour of your West Indian colleague is lawful.

There is also a general rule that no complaint can be made about special treatment given to members of any racial group if that treatment is designed to meet their special needs in regard to education, training, welfare or any ancillary benefit. For example:

vii   You are a white worker at a factory which employs many Asian workers. The factory owners lay on special courses for those Asian workers who have difficulty in reading or writing English. You cannot read or write and you apply to be included in these courses but the employer refuses. You have no claim under the Race Relations Act.

It is important to note that these limited measures of positive discrimination are permitted, but are not compulsory. If you were the West Indian store assistant in Example vi you would have no complaint if the employer refused to give you preferential treatment and considered your application strictly on its merits. If you were one of the Asian workers in Example vii and the employer decided not to lay on special language courses then there would be nothing that you could do about it.

Recognising and proving direct discrimination

In order to succeed in your claim against your employer you will have to show that the employer was influenced by your colour or some other racial factor. When we say employer, this does not necessarily mean the owner of the business but the person who actually made the decision as to whether you should be offered promotion. For example this could be a department head or personnel manager rather than the owner of the business.

It may not be enough to prove that you were more suitable for promotion than the employee who was actually offered the promotion. However, if you can show this then you will be a long way towards winning your case. If you can show that you were more suitable and the employer cannot give the industrial tribunal any explanation which they find acceptable then the tribunal are likely to find the case proved. However, if the employer gives a reason which the tribunal accept to be genuine, then they will dismiss your claim, even if in the employer's shoes they would have come to a different decision. For example:

viii You are of Indian origin. You and a white colleague apply for promotion to a more senior post which has become vacant. The choice between you is made by the head of the department. He chooses your white colleague, even though you have better qualifications and more experience. You complain that the failure to promote you amounts to racial discrimination and your claim is heard by an industrial tribunal. The department head, when he gives evidence, is asked why he preferred the other applicant, in view of your superior qualifications and experience. He says that he decided against you because of your record of unpunctuality. The members of the tribunal, if they had been making the appointment, would not have regarded your record as being so bad as to outweigh your superior qualifications and experience. However, they believe the department head when he says that this was genuinely the reason why he decided against you and that he was in no way influenced by your colour or ethnic origin. Accordingly your claim fails.

False reason

If on the other hand the reason given for not promoting you is one that is obviously or probably false, then the employer may be in a worse position than if no reason at all had been given. The tribunal members will be ready to draw the conclusion that if a false reason has been put forward that is because the true reason is your colour or some other racial ground. For example:

ix   Your parents came to England from Pakistan. You work for a large organisation. A post in a more senior grade becomes vacant. It is the usual practice for vacancies in that grade to be filled by the most senior employee working in your grade. A panel of senior officers of the organisation interview you for the post but offer the appointment to a white man who is junior to you. You complain that this is racial discrimination and at the tribunal hearing the members of the appointments panel who give evidence say that they decided against you because you have difficulty in communicating effectively in English. The tribunal members were able to judge for themselves when you gave evidence that you speak perfect English. Accordingly they do not accept that the reason given by the members of the appointments panel is the true reason and they uphold your complaint.

When you are denied a chance of promotion you are in one respect better able to judge for yourself whether this may be on racial grounds than you could if you were applying for the job as an outsider. If you apply for a job from outside you are likely to know nothing about the successful applicant. If on the other hand you and someone who works at the same place are both after promotion, you are likely to know quite a lot about your competitor. Even if you do not work side by side, it will often be possible to find out, from friends who do work with him, how good he is at his job and what his qualifications are. If you can see for yourself or are told by your friends that he is better at his job than you are, or better qualified, or has been with the company longer, then this may satisfy you that he has been promoted on his merits and not because he is white and you are black or brown. If on the other hand he seems to be a less suitable candidate for promotion than you are, then you may suspect racial discrimination and wish to take the matter further.

You may still face the difficulty that you do not know what influenced the person or group of people at the company who decided against you and in favour of the other candidate for promotion. If you approach the person who made the decision or your immediate superior in order to find out what the reason was, he or she may refuse to give you a reason. Even if a reason is given to you you may not know whether or not that reason is true. Must you then either let the matter drop or take your case to the industrial tribunal, knowing that when you get to the tribunal hearing there may be some perfectly good explanation for the decision not to promote you?

The questions procedure

There is another step open to you. Before deciding whether to take your case to an industrial tribunal you can send your employer the form of questionnaire for which the Race Relations Act makes provision. Details about where to obtain this questionnaire and when it has to be sent to the employer are contained in Chapter 5. In the questionnaire you will tell the employer that you suspect that the failure to promote you may have been an act of racial discrimination and you will ask the employer why you were not offered the promotion. If the employer refuses to answer or gives an answer which later turns out to be false or deliberately misleading then this will greatly strengthen your case.

Documents

It would usually be very foolish for the employer to give false answers in the reply to the questionnaire. When a decision is made between two candidates for promotion, a number of documents will normally be considered by the person or persons making the appointment. They could, for example, ask for written reports from your department head. They may look at annual reports from your superior on your performance and potential and similar reports in respect of the other candidate. Even though these are all confidential documents the tribunal will normally be prepared to order the employer to produce them, whenever it is essential for the tribunal to see the documents in order to do justice to your case. The employer would also be required to produce other documents which are directly relevant to the case, such as the notes made at your interview and those made when the successful candidate was interviewed.

Racial hostility

Sometimes you will have more direct evidence that there has been racial discrimination against you. If the industrial tribunal members are satisfied that one of the people who has made the decision not to promote you has shown racial hostility towards you then the tribunal are likely to find in your favour. It does not matter whether the hostility was shown before the question of the promotion came up, at the interview for the promotion or subsequently. For example:

x   You are of West Indian origin and you work in a large office with a white colleague. You are both in the same grade. You both apply for promotion to a higher grade. The office manager is always friendly in his manner towards your white colleague but very offhand in his manner towards you. It is your white colleague who is offered the promotion to the higher grade. When you ask the office manager why you had been unsuccessful he tells you that he is not prepared to bandy words with the like of you and says that "You people are never satisfied. You should be grateful that you have a job at all." If the tribunal members believe your evidence about the office manager's attitude before the promotion came up and about what he said afterwards then they are likely to decide that his decision not to promote you was made on racial grounds.

Further evidence of racial hostility by a person involved in the decision not to promote you may be obtained if the employer is ordered to produce confidential documents about you. If reports on you by this person contain remarks which are derogatory and unjustifiable then these may also amount to evidence of discrimination.

If the tribunal are satisfied that a decision not to offer you promotion was made on racial grounds, the employer cannot defeat your claim by showing that the decision was made under duress.

Prejudice by other people, whether fellow workers or customers, can never be an acceptable excuse for racial discrimination. For example:

xi   You are an experienced and competent shop floor worker, popular with most of your colleagues. You are of African origin. You apply for promotion to a vacant post as a foreman, but a small group of your fellow workers, including the union shop steward, tell the company that they are not prepared to work under a black man and that if you are promoted the company will have a strike on its hands. The company gives way to this pressure and you are told that unfortunately you cannot be offered the promotion to foreman. You take your case to an industrial tribunal and are able to prove that the decision not to promote you was made because of the threats by some of your white colleagues. The company can have no defence to your claim.

One defence which may sometimes be put forward by employers is that if there were any racial discrimination in the company then you would have not been offered the job there in the first place. This is not usually a very convincing defence. First of all the person who decided to offer you a job with the company may not be the same person as the one who decided not to offer you promotion. Secondly, a form which racial prejudice sometimes takes is to regard black or brown people as being suitable for menial jobs but unsuitable for promotion to more responsible or demanding posts.

Indirect discrimination

Most complaints about discrimination in the selection of employees for promotion or training are complaints of direct discrimination. We have already seen that if in reply to such a complaint your employer falsely says that you were turned down because of language difficulties, then by giving this false reason the employer is giving you evidence of direct discrimination. But what if the employer genuinely refuses to consider you for promotion because you cannot communicate well in English? If you belong to an ethnic minority group, you will probably have little difficulty in satisfying the tribunal that this language requirement bars a much greater proportion of the members of your racial group than of employees not belonging to that racial group. In order to defeat your claim the employer then has to show that the requirement is a justifiable one. If the job which you are after does not involve much more need to communicate than your present one does then the employer will have great difficulty in defeating your claim. For example:

xii   You are a lady from Bangladesh working as a junior laboratory technician. You apply for promotion to a more senior post in the laboratory. The new job would be more demanding and responsible (and better paid) than your present job but, like your present job, would be an entirely technical job and would not involve you in any managerial function or any extra need to communicate with your fellow employees. The company refuses to consider you for the promotion because you do not speak English well enough. If you were to complain of racial discrimination the company would have great difficulty in showing the language requirement to be justifiable.

If on the other hand the job which you are after involves some sort of managerial or personnel work or dealing with the public, then it may be comparatively easy for the employer to show that a language requirement is justifiable. For example:

xiii   You are of Indian origin and you work as a clerk in an office, dealing with correspondence. You read and write English perfectly but you still have some difficulty in making yourself understood when speaking English. You apply for promotion to the post of office manager, which is a job which will involve supervision of and communication with your fellow employees rather than paper work. Your employers refuse to consider the application because of your inability to communicate well when speaking English. It is likely that because of the kind of work involved the industrial tribunal would regard the requirement as justifiable.

Another kind of requirement which may lead to a claim of indirect discrimination is a requirement that to be considered for promotion you must have a degree or some other educational qualification. The employer may be unable to justify this sort of requirement if the employer is insisting on qualifications obtained in the United Kingdom and is unwilling to consider equivalent qualifications obtained overseas. The requirement could also be unjustifiable if it is excessive and unreasonable bearing in mind the kind of job involved and your suitability in other respects for the job. For example:

xiv   You are of West Indian origin. You are a very experienced and successful sales representative and apply for promotion to the post of sales manager. The company has a policy that it will not consider promoting people to posts at this level unless they have a university degree. You cannot meet this requirement because you have no degree. It is unlikely that the company would be able to satisfy an industrial tribunal that this requirement is justifiable, because the requirement has little to do with a person's suitability for the job.

It has recently been decided by the courts (see the Introduction, page 5) that you cannot complain about your employer taking account of some factor, whether or not directly relevant to the job, if this is only one of the factors taken into account and is not a rigid requirement. If, in the last example, the employer had genuinely considered you for the job, but had preferred a rather less experienced applicant for the job because he had a degree, then there would have been no indirect discrimination. It is only when the employer refuses even to consider you for the promotion because you cannot comply with some requirement that the question of indirect discrimination arises.

7

Other forms of discrimination at work

The most common complaints of discrimination at work, apart from those about promotion and training, are complaints that the employer has discriminated in dismissing you or in giving you all the unpleasant jobs at work or subjecting you to racial abuse or harassment. It is also forbidden however for the employer to discriminate in fixing your wage or any other term of your employment or any fringe benefit.

Wages

It is unusual for a member of an ethnic minority to complain that he or she is being paid a lower wage than the wage which would be paid if he or she were white. However, the question of indirect discrimination could possibly arise if you are a female part-time worker. For example:

i   You are a West Indian lady and you work part-time in a factory. You would not be able to work full-time because you have children at home. The wage which you are paid for each hour that you work is less than the wage which the full-time workers are paid for each hour that they work. You are able to prove that virtually all the West Indian ladies working at the factory are part-time workers, because they all have children at home, but a much higher proportion of the other female workers are childless and are able to work full-time. Accordingly, the employer's requirement that in order to earn the higher rate per hour you should work full-time is one that you cannot comply with and it is also one that affects a considerably greater proportion of the West Indian women than of the other women. If your work involves operating some particular machine which stands idle when you are not at work then the employer could perhaps justify the higher hourly rate for full-time workers. If, however, you are doing some work like packing and the employer gets as much value for each hour that you work as he does for each hour that the full-time workers put in then you may well succeed in a claim of indirect discrimination. However, if you do you can expect to come away with nothing more than a declaration from the tribunal that the discrimination against you is unlawful and that the employer should change his practice of having differential wage rates for part-time and full-time workers. You would not be awarded any compensation, because the employer would have no difficulty in showing that the difference in wage rates was not deliberately intended to enable him to pay lower wages to West Indian workers.

Fringe benefits

You can complain about discrimination by an employer denying you some benefit, even if there is nothing in your contract that gives you a right to that benefit. For example:

ii   You are a senior white administrator, working with an Indian assistant. It is the usual practice of your employer to send administrators of your rank to conferences twice a year at the employer's expense. However, instead the employer sends your assistant, in order to demonstrate how enlightened the employer is by employing members of ethnic minorities at such high levels in the organisation. This racial discrimination against you is unlawful.

However, you must be careful not to waste the time of an industrial tribunal with a complaint which a tribunal would regard as frivolous. For example:

iii   You are a coloured office worker and you eat in the company canteen with all the other office workers, white and coloured, except the directors. They, who are all white, have their own dining room. You would like to eat in the directors' dining room and you complain that this is indirect discrimination because the requirement that to eat in the directors' dining room you must be

99

a director is one that only white employees can comply with. An industrial tribunal would have little difficulty in finding that the requirement was justifiable and your claim unfounded.

Unpleasant jobs and racial abuse

If your foreman, because of his racial hostility or prejudice, gives you all the unpleasant jobs, then you will have a claim against both your employer and the foreman. The employer is responsible for the foreman's actions unless it can show that it has an equal opportunity policy and has genuinely made all practicable efforts to enforce this policy. It is no good the directors simply resolving that the company should be an equal opportunity employer and then doing nothing more about the policy. If there is a code of practice in force under the Race Relations Act the tribunal will expect the employer to have taken the steps recommended in that code.

You may still have a claim against your employer even if it is in the interests of good industrial relations that you are given the less pleasant work. For example:

iv   You work in a factory that employs mainly white workers. One of them is always picking on you and insulting you because of your colour. The white worker is transferred by your employer. You are also transferred, even though you are blameless. The employer does this because he feels that the other white workers could be upset if the white man were transferred and you were not. Your new job has the same pay and status as your old job but less pleasant working conditions. You can complain of direct racial discrimination. Even though you have been treated in the same way as the white man who was picking on you, you have still been treated badly on racial grounds, because a white worker in your position, who had been picked on by a colleague and was himself blameless, would not have been transferred.

Segregation

The Race Relations Act specifically provides that segregation on racial grounds is racial discrimination. If the employer were to insist on all the workers in some ethnic group being on the same shift then this would be direct racial discrimination. It is also unlawful for an employer to insist on segregation in the use of a canteen or toilets or in any other way.

Dismissal

Even if you are dismissed for your admitted misconduct, the question of discrimination could arise. For example:

v   You are of West Indian origin. You and a white worker have been caught fighting. You are both equally to blame. You both have bad records for fighting and there is nothing to choose between your two records. You are dismissed but the white worker is let off with a warning. By treating you worse than your white colleague the employer has directly discriminated against you, unless the employer can show that there is some reason other than the difference in colour for singling you out for dismissal.

It is also unlawful for an employer to dismiss you (or treat you unfavourably in any other way) because you have made a complaint or supported another worker's complaint under the Race Relations Act. For example:

vi   You are a white office worker. An Indian colleague complains that he has been denied promotion on racial grounds and you give evidence for him at the industrial tribunal hearing. Your evidence is honest and is given in good faith. A few months later the company has to make a number of employees redundant. You are selected for redundancy and colleagues in the same grade who have been with the company for a much shorter period are kept on. Unless the company can give some satisfactory explanation for selecting you for redundancy instead of your colleagues with less service an industrial tribunal would be ready to conclude that you were being victimised for having given evidence against the company and you would be awarded compensation.

The above example illustrates that even in a redundancy situation the question of direct discrimination in dismissals can arise. There

101

must be no victimisation and selection for redundancy must be made on strictly non-racial grounds.

Quite often selection for redundancy is made on the "last in, first out" principle. If you are a new employee then you are more likely to be dismissed when the need for redundancy arises. This rule could apparently be indirectly discriminatory when a company has only recently started taking on coloured workers. However, it is likely that an industrial tribunal would find the rule to be justifiable, since it is an established principle in industrial relations and in the bargaining between employers and unions.

What if you are dismissed on racial grounds only a few months or even weeks after you have joined the company? Can you do anything about it, bearing in mind that where there is no racial discrimination involved you can complain about unfair dismissal only if you have worked for at least a year for the employer? The rule is that there is no minimum period for which you have to work before you can complain about racial discrimination. If you are given a job and then dismissed on your first day, for instance because of pressure from some of your fellow workers, you can take your case to an industrial tribunal and claim compensation. It does not matter how long you have been with the employer or what age you are.

If you are dismissed from your job on racial grounds and are successful in your claim against the employer then the amount of compensation awarded to you may be very substantial, very much more than in most other claims of racial discrimination against employers. The amount will depend partly on how long you have been with the employer, partly on the time you are out of work before the tribunal hearing and partly on your prospects of obtaining another job in the future. If you have been with the employer for a number of years and if you have been out of work since being dismissed and if you are unlikely to obtain another job then the compensation could be very substantial indeed, running into several thousand pounds. In addition to compensation for your actual financial losses and anticipated financial losses in the future you are also entitled to compensation for the injury to your feelings. This compensation for injury to feelings is payable whenever there is a successful claim of direct racial discrimination. It can be very hurtful to be treated unfavourably on racial grounds and this is something for which you are entitled to compensation, although the amounts awarded by industrial tribunals tend to be fairly modest.

There is one further point which you should always bear in mind if you have a claim of discrimination arising from your dismissal. The longer you are out of work the larger your claim is likely to be. However, you must be able to show the industrial tribunal that you have done all that you reasonably can to find alternative work. In any claim you are under a duty to take all reasonable steps to mitigate your loss. If you simply sit at home deliberately failing to apply for jobs and refusing to attend for interviews and even turning down jobs offered to you then the industrial tribunal will be unsympathetic. The tribunal will make an assumption as to the earliest time at which you could have found a new job had you really tried and will fix the compensation accordingly.

Exceptions

In the last chapter we considered a few circumstances in which discrimination against you relating to promotion or training may sometimes be permitted. The exception when you are employed for the purposes of a private household also applies to any other form of discrimination at work. If, for example, you are employed as a maid or gardener at a private house and, on racial grounds, you are paid a lower wage or given all the unpleasant jobs, there is nothing you can do about it. If you are dismissed from such a job on racial grounds you have no claim under the Race Relations Act, although you could have a claim for unfair dismissal under the Employment Protection (Consolidation) Act 1978. As mentioned in earlier chapters, even if you are employed for the purposes of a private household you could have a claim if you are victimised for having taken or supported some action under the Race Relations Act. Also the exception does not apply to contract workers.

There are one or two other exceptions in the Act which are not of great general importance. If you are employed on a ship and you applied for the job or were engaged outside Great Britain then you will have no claim in respect of any form of discrimination against you by your employer. This exception does not apply to workers from overseas who are employed on oil rigs or on doing other exploration work in certain designated areas.

We saw in Chapter 2 that you can have no claim under the Act if you are not appointed to a statutory office, such as that of a justice of the peace. You can also have no claim under the Act if you are deprived of such an office, even if you are sure that the decision has been taken on racial grounds. You can also have no claim if you are a non-executive company director without a service contract and you are removed from the board on racial grounds, because you do not fall within the definition of an employee.

If you are not in domestic service and you are not a sailor from overseas or a justice of the peace or a non-executive company director then there are unlikely to be any circumstances in which the forms of discrimination against you considered in this chapter will be lawful.

8

What you should do about discrimination by your employer

You should read the whole of Chapter 5, as well as this chapter, because most of the advice given there applies to claims against your employer as well as to claims against somebody who has refused to employ you. There are some additional points which need to be considered when your claim is against your employer and these points are dealt with in this chapter.

Time limits

The time limit is the same, whether you are complaining about your own employer or about somebody who has refused to employ you. Your originating application IT 1 must be received at the Tribunal Central Office within three months after the date of the act of discrimination complained of.

Sometimes you may not be sure of the date of the act of discrimination against you. For example:

i   You are black. The head of your department leaves on 1st February 1983. Your employer does not invite formal applications for the post, but you expect to be considered. On 1st March 1983 you learn that a less qualified white colleague of yours has been offered the post. You do not know on what date during February the decision was made to promote your colleague. You do not know on what date the post was offered to him. To be on the safe side, you should assume that the three months starts from 1st February and make sure that your originating application is received at the Central Office before the end of April 1983, even though in fact you may have more time than that.

If you are complaining about discrimination in dismissing you, you should make sure that your originating application is received at the Central Office within three months after you are told that you are to be dismissed, even though the effective date of dismissal may be later than that date. Strictly speaking it could be argued that the act of discrimination occurs when you are told that you are to be dismissed and not when any notice given to you expires.

What if you are not complaining about a single act of discrimination but about something which is going on over a period? For example, you are, on racial grounds, being paid a lower wage than your colleagues. You can present your claim to an industrial tribunal at any time whilst this continuous discrimination against you continues or within three months after the discrimination ceases.

What if the thing which you are complaining about has happened before? For example:

ii   Your application for promotion has been turned down and you believe that this was on racial grounds. You applied for promotion a year ago and you feel that this application was also turned down on racial grounds. You complain to a tribunal about the recent discrimination. Does the three months time limit mean that you can say nothing at all about the previous refusal to promote you? Although your formal complaint is about the recent refusal to promote you and that is the one which you are seeking compensation for, you can give evidence about the previous incident in order to add weight to your complaint. If you have been passed over once in favour of a fellow employee who is less qualified and less experienced the employer may have some good explanation for the decision, but if this has happened more than once then the employer will find it more difficult to give a satisfactory explanation.

Help with your case

Everything that was said in Chapter 5 about the value of having expert help, for example from the Commission or a solicitor, to present your complaint applies also where the complaint is against your employer.

As you are in work, you may belong to a trade union. The union may be able to send someone along to present your case for you at the hearing or to pay for a solicitor to do so and you should approach the union if the Commission for Racial Equality is unable or unwilling to assist you. A union official who is experienced in these matters may be able to present your case at the tribunal hearing much better than you could yourself. He does not need to be legally qualified in order to represent you. The same goes for your local Community Relations Officer if he is willing to represent you.

Trying to settle your case

Most employers, especially large organisations, have a procedure for dealing with grievances by their employees. For example, if you want to complain about something which your foreman has done, you may have a right of appeal or complaint to the works manager. Usually the employer's grievance procedure will include provision for you to take along a workmate or a shop steward to help you put your case over to the employer.

It is vital for three reasons that, whilst keeping your eye on the three months time limit, you should use the employer's own grievance procedure before you take your case to an industrial tribunal. First of all, what you are really after will usually be for the employer to change the decision which has been made, not for compensation to be paid. If you have been refused promotion or training, you probably still want that promotion or training, not just money to compensate you for not having it. The employer is more likely to be favourably disposed towards you and to hear your complaint sympathetically if you have used the company's internal grievance procedure and not rushed off to haul the employer before an industrial tribunal. Furthermore, if you use the company's grievance procedure right away it may be possible to put the matter right immediately. For example, if you are complaining about having been left off a training course, there may still be a place on the training course which could be offered to you.

Secondly, if as a result of taking up your grievance with the company you are given a satisfactory explanation for what has happened, then you will have saved both yourself and the company the trouble of having to go along to a tribunal hearing. For example:

iii You feel that your foreman is giving you all the difficult jobs to do and you believe that this could be because of the colour of your skin. He has refused to give you any explanation. You take up your complaint with the company, using the grievance procedure. You find out that it has been decided to consider you for promotion to a higher grade and that the foreman has been instructed to test your ability to do more difficult and responsible work, without telling you why.

Thirdly, if you take your case to an industrial tribunal, two of the three tribunal members hearing your case will have knowledge or experience of industry and they will be surprised, and possibly unsympathetic to you, if you have taken your case straight to the tribunal without using the grievance procedure first and giving your employer a chance to put the matter right.

Even after you have sent off your originating application to the Tribunal Central Office you should still be willing to discuss the possibility of settling your claim. What is said in Chapter 5, about ACAS conciliation officers, is also relevant to claims against employers.

The questions procedure

The questionnaire is less important than it is in cases where you are complaining about being turned down for a job or not offered an interview, because when your complaint is against your own employer you will know a lot more about the circumstances than you do when you are complaining about somebody who has refused to employ you. If, for example, you are complaining about discrimination in refusing to promote you, you will usually know something about the successful candidate for promotion.

However, you should still use the questionnaire in order to find out, for instance, why the employer has decided to dismiss you or not to promote you. For example:

iv You are one of four assistants in a shop. The shop manager leaves and you and one of the other assistants apply for the vacancy. You have been there much longer than the other assistant but she is appointed. You think that this may be because you are black and she is white. You approach the owner of the shop but he refuses to discuss the matter with you. You then obtain the form of questionnaire under the Race Relations Act, fill in the questions which you wish to be answered and send the form to your employer. In his reply the employer denies discrimination and states that he promoted the other assistant instead of you because you tend to be difficult and obstructive with customers when they try to return faulty goods. Before you decide whether to take your case to an industrial tribunal you must consider whether the employer could be right in what he is saying about you and whether that could genuinely be the reason why you have not been promoted.

When filling in question 2 on the form, you should make clear what sort of treatment you are complaining about, such as dismissal or failure to promote you, but you should not set this out in great detail in the way in which you would when giving evidence, you should not speculate about the reasons for your treatment and you should not take this opportunity of releasing all your pent up frustration and resentment against your employer. You are using the form to seek information, not to prove to your employer that you have been discriminated against. You should not say very much when filling in question 3 which is the one beginning with the words "I consider that this treatment may have been unlawful because". You could simply cross out the word "because" and then ignore this question.

If you have been dismissed then, whether or not you use the questions procedure, you should write to the employer asking for the reason for your dismissal. The employer must given you the reason within 14 days.

Sending off the originating application

The form IT 1 is the same whether you are complaining about discrimination as an applicant for a job or as an employee, but if you are an employee there are a few extra details to be filled in. For example, you need to answer questions 7, 8, 9 and 10, which ask about the date when your employment began (and the date when it ended if you have been dismissed or left), your basic wage and your average take home pay, any other renumeration or benefits and your normal basic weekly hours of work.

If you have been dismissed, then in question 1 you should put "Racial discrimination and unfair dismissal". Then in question 14 you should state "reinstatement" if you wish to have your job back.

Do not worry too much about question 11 if you are not sure of the date of the act of discrimination. In example i at the beginning of this chapter you could put 1st March 1983, being the date when you became aware that somebody else had been promoted, not you. When you are complaining about continuous discrimination, for example relating to your rate of pay, you could put "continuously up to present date".

The advice given in Chapter 5 about questions 12 and 13 also applies here. You should make it clear what kind of treatment you are complaining about but you should not give more detail than is necessary at this stage.

Further particulars

In his reply to your questionnaire or in his notice of appearance in his response to your application to the tribunal the employer may give an explanation for the way in which you have been treated. For example, he may say that you have been overlooked for promotion because you are incompetent or that you have been dismissed because of some misconduct. You should always ask for further particulars of any allegation of this kind.

If you are going to be represented at the hearing it is important that you should discuss very fully and frankly with your representative any suggestions of incompetence or misconduct that could be made against you. It will be far easier for your representative to deal with any allegations against you and put them in perspective if he or she knows what you have to say about them well in advance rather than if he or she is faced with them, without any prior warning, at the tribunal hearing itself.

Documents

It is particularly important when you have a claim against your employer that all relevant documents should be available at the tribunal hearing. You will probably wish to compare the way that you have been treated with the way that the employer has treated an employee of a different colour or ethnic group. The documents which may be relevant will include written appraisals or assessments of you or reports on you made by one of your superiors, similar documents relating to the employee with whom you are comparing yourself and sometimes documents like work sheets. As mentioned in the Introduction and in Chapter 5, when you need these documents to prove your case, the employer will not usually be allowed to keep them back on the ground that they are confidential.

Witnesses

It may be necessary at the tribunal hearing for you to ask the tribunal to compare you with one of your colleagues, for instance a person who has been promoted whilst you have not. It may be difficult for you to be objective about your own qualities and abilities and it is always useful to have a reliable witness who can support your own evidence. For example:

v   You are of Indian origin and you are working at an office with a white colleague who is rather less qualified and experienced. A senior post in the department becomes vacant and it is your white colleague who is promoted. A senior person working in the department is willing to give evidence that you are more hard working and efficient than the white man who has been promoted and also that the head of the department, who has made the decision, has consistently shown a hostile and unfriendly attitude towards you and given you the less pleasant jobs to do. This evidence, if accepted by the tribunal, will make it more likely that they will make a finding of racial discrimination.

A fellow employee who wants to give evidence on your behalf may be worried about the possible consequences to himself or herself. What if he or she were to damage his or her own promotion prospects or even to be dismissed for having given evidence against the employer? There are provisions in the Race Relations Act to prevent victimisation. An employee who is denied promotion or in any other way treated unfavourably because he or she has given evidence against the employer has the same right to claim compensation as he or she would have if he or she had been treated unfavourably on racial grounds.

There is one exception. If an employee who gives evidence for you is not acting in good faith but is trying to harm the employer, because of some personal grievance, then the victimisation provisions will not apply. It will in any event be damaging rather than helpful to your case if you are relying on a witness who is clearly motivated not by a desire to see justice done but by personal ill-will against the employer. The best possible witness in support of your complaint would be a fellow employee who is contented and conscientious and loyal to the employer but who is compelled to come forward to give evidence because of concern about the unfair way in which you have been treated.

Your colleague may also be worried about losing money by attending the tribunal hearing. You should point out that immediately after the hearing arrangements can be made with the tribunal clerk to make a claim for travelling expenses and subsistence and loss of earnings allowances.

If a lawyer (or a complaints officer from the Commission for Racial Equality or some other person) is going to be appearing on your behalf at the tribunal hearing, you should arrange for him or her to see your witness as soon as possible. If you will be conducting your own case, you should ask the witness for a full written statement of the evidence which he or she will be giving at the hearing. It is always important, in any kind of court or tribunal hearing, to know in advance what the witnesses you will be calling intend to say.

In order to attend the tribunal hearing and give evidence your witness will need time off from work. The employer should be asked as soon as possible for an assurance that the witness will be given time off to attend the hearing. If the employer is obstructive, then you (or your lawyer or other representative if you have one) should write to the local tribunal office dealing with your case giving the name and address of the witness and explaining the circumstances and asking for an order requiring the attendance of the witness.

Remedies

The advice given in Chapter 5 about the tribunal hearing need not be repeated here. However, you should very carefully consider in advance whether you wish the tribunal to make any recommendation, if you win your case. If you have been passed over for promotion, have any further senior posts become vacant or are any senior employees about to retire? If so, do you wish the tribunal to make a recommendation that you should be appointed to one of those vacancies? If your complaint is about hostile treatment by your immediate superior, do you wish the tribunal to recommend that either you or your superior should be moved to some other department, section or shift?

If you have been dismissed, do you wish to be reinstated? If so, is your old job still available or have any other suitable jobs become vacant?

Summary of Chapter 8

Some of the most important points to consider, as well as those mentioned in Chapter 5, when you have a claim against your employer, are as follows:

1. Always make use of any internal grievance procedure, as long as you can do so and still be sure that your originating application is received at the Tribunal Central Office within three months.
2. If you have been dismissed, mention unfair dismissal as well as racial discrimination in question 1 of your originating application.
3. Ask for production of any relevant documents, including confidential documents which could explain the difference in your treatment and that of a fellow employee.
4. It will be helpful if you can take along as a witness a reliable colleague from work.
5. Consider very carefully what you could say in answer to any allegations of misconduct or incompetence against you.
6. Consider before the hearing whether you wish the tribunal to make any recommendations for your benefit, such as reinstatement, if you win your case.

Part III

Discrimination to do with houses and flats

You have rights under the Race Relations Act when you make an offer for a house or flat, when you apply for a loan to assist you in your purchase, when you try to obtain rented accommodation and when you have become a tenant. We shall see that there are very few circumstances in which racial discrimination against you is permitted.

These rights are considered in Chapters 10, 11, 12 and 13. First of all Chapter 9 explains briefly what steps you should take when you have a complaint to do with housing.

9

What to do about your complaint

When you want to complain about discrimination to do with your job or a job application, your case will be heard by an industrial tribunal. Other cases are heard by a county court judge. When you have to take your complaint to a county court, it is both easier and more important to have a lawyer to put your case than it is when your complaint is one for an industrial tribunal to deal with.

It is important to have legal representation for two main reasons. The first is that the proceedings at a county court hearing are more formal than an industrial tribunal hearing and you would find it more difficult to present your own case effectively. The second reason is that if you lose your case and you are not legally aided you would normally be ordered to pay the costs of your opponent. If he has been represented by a solicitor or barrister, these costs could amount to a lot of money. The order for you to pay the costs will be made even if you genuinely thought that you had a good case and even if you acted reasonably in starting the proceedings.

Legal representation

Where should you look for legal representation? One possibility is to apply for legal aid. This is the second important difference between county court proceedings and industrial tribunal hearings. For county court proceedings legal aid is available. If your income is low enough and you can show reasonable grounds for taking proceedings you should be able to obtain legal advice and representation. Go to a solicitor and ask for initial advice, which could be free, under the "green form" scheme. Ask the solicitor to help you to fill in a legal aid application form. If your application is granted, you will be told either that you will have full legal aid, without having to make any financial contribution yourself, or that your own financial contribution will be limited to a specified amount. The legal aid will enable you to have a solicitor to deal with the preparation of your case and a solicitor or barrister to represent you at the hearing itself.

The other main possibility is to approach the Commission for Racial Equality. They may be willing to pay for a solicitor or arrange for one of their own complaints officers to handle your case and to represent you at the court hearing. Even if they are not prepared to assist you to that extent, they will usually give you initial advice about your claim.

A third possibility is to go to a law centre, if there is one in your area and a fourth is to approach your local CRO.

You could explore all possibilities, by approaching the Commission or the local CRO first and then going to see a solicitor or to a law centre if the Commission indicate that they are unlikely to be able to offer you full representation.

Time limits

Whatever you do, you must do it quickly. The proceedings must be commenced within six months after the discrimination which you wish to complain about. If you have applied to the Commission for Racial Equality for help this period will be extended to eight months. You should not wait until the six months are nearly up before you do anything about your complaint. You should go and see a solicitor or the Commission right away, so that your application for legal aid or your formal application to the Commission for help can be dealt with before the time for commencing proceedings expires. If you formally apply to the Commission for help they have two months in which to reply. They can write to you, before the two months are up, extending by a further month both their time for replying and your own time for commencing proceedings.

Questionnaires and documents

When you see a solicitor or the Commission, one of the first things to be discussed will be a questionnaire to be sent to the defendant, the person whom you wish to complain against. This is the special form of questionnaire (mentioned in the Introduction) under the Race Relations Act. It must be sent to the defendant before you actually commence proceedings. Examples will be given in some of the next four chapters about the kind of questions that you may find it useful to ask. If the defendant refuses to answer or gives evasive answers, this could go against him at the hearing.

You should also discuss with your solicitor or the Commission whether there are any documents which you or the defendant may wish to refer to at the hearing. You must produce at the hearing any relevant documents which you have. You in turn can require the defendant to produce any relevant documents which are in his possession. If he refuses, your solicitor will be able to ask the court beforehand for an order requiring the production of the documents. The court may order the defendant to produce documents which are confidential, provided that this is essential in order to do justice to your case. It is important to discuss this question of documents with your solicitor or the Commission at an early stage and certainly well before the hearing.

You should also, when you first see your solicitor or the Commission, give the name and address of any witness whose evidence could help your case.

The hearing itself

At the hearing, your solicitor or barrister will make an opening speech. Then you and any witnesses you may have will give evidence. You will be questioned by your own solicitor or barrister, then by the solicitor or barrister acting for the defendant and then again by your own solicitor or barrister. It will then be the turn of the defendant and his witnesses to give their evidence.

The case will be heard by a county court judge. He or she will sit with two assessors who have specialised knowledge of race relations. However, the judge alone will decide whether you have made out your case, and if so, what order should be made.

What can the court do for you?

If you win your case, the judge will declare that the defendant has acted unlawfully towards you. You will usually be entitled to damages. These will include compensation for any financial loss which you have suffered or are likely to suffer. The judge may also award compensation for the injury to your feelings.

Compensation cannot be awarded if the complaint is one of indirect discrimination and the defendant can show that the discrimination was not racially motivated.

The judge can also grant an injunction, ordering the defendant to stop discriminating against you or not to discriminate against you again. In practice injunctions are rarely granted in discrimination cases.

Appeals

The losing party, whether you or the defendant, can appeal on a point of law to the Court of Appeal. Occasionally there can be a further appeal to the House of Lords.

10

Buying a house or flat

The general rule is that a person who has a house or flat to sell must not discriminate against you either by refusing to sell to you or by offering to sell to you at a higher price or on stiffer terms than would be offered to someone of a different racial group. Estate agents must not discriminate either, and if they do you could have a claim against both the agent and the person selling the property.

The exception to the rule

Racial discrimination against you is allowed if the house is being sold by an owner occupier and he is not using an agent and not advertising the sale in any way. Advertising is defined in very broad terms. It includes not only newspaper advertising but also putting up a board in the garden or a card in the window.

This exception is not often likely to be important in practice, because if a person is selling a house or flat to someone he knows and is not using either an agent or any kind of advertising then it is most unlikely that you will ever come to hear that the property is for sale and want to make an offer for it.

There is one other exception to the general rule but it is also one which you will rarely come across in practice. If a person is selling a flat and either he or a relative occupies a flat in the same building, then discrimination against you could be lawful if the person occupying the other flat would be sharing some kind of living accommodation (not storage accommodation) with you. It is however fairly rare for a flat to be sold rather than rented when there is shared living accommodation.

Recognising and proving discrimination

Not many people with a house or flat to sell would want to turn down
your offer for the property in order to take a lower offer from someone
of a different colour. Few people are so devoted to their prejudices that
they wish to make financial sacrifices for them. It is important to
understand that sharp practice and unfair behaviour are not
necessarily evidence of racial discrimination. For example:

i   You are black. You see a house advertised in the paper and make
      an offer of £20,000. The vendor agrees to accept this offer and
      you shake hands on the deal. A week later you are told by the
      vendor that another person has offered £21,000 and that he
      intends to accept this offer unless you can match it. You cannot
      afford the extra money and you have to let the house go. Even
      though the vendor has not treated you fairly, there has been no
      racial discrimination against you, provided that he was
      influenced not by the colour of your skin but by greed for more
      money.

There are two ways in which discrimination in the sale of houses or
flats does sometimes happen in practice. First of all, a person selling his
property may be subjected to pressure from his neighbours not to sell
to a black or brown person. It is no defence for a person who
discriminates to say that he has done so not because he is personally
prejudiced but because somebody else has persuaded or forced him to
discriminate. For example:

ii   You have a brown skin. You agree to buy a house from a man
      who has a shop a few streets away. Before the contract is signed
      you receive a telephone call from the vendor of the house. He is
      very embarrassed. He tells you that he is having to back out of
      the sale because his white neighbours have told him that if he
      sells the house to a coloured person they will stop using his shop
      and make sure that all their friends do the same. You can take
      proceedings against the vendor in the county court and claim
      damages. He will have no defence to your claim even though the
      discrimination was really against his will. You cannot personally
      take any action against the neighbours, but you should report all
      the circumstances to the Commission for Racial Equality so that

122

the Commission can then consider taking action.

You may also face racial discrimination if you want to buy a house on an estate and the developer or agent has adjoining houses for sale. If the agent feels that white people may be put off buying the adjoining houses by having the prospect of a black or brown neighbour, you may be given some false excuse for the property not being available.

The questionnaire procedure

If you feel that you may have suffered racial discrimination in this way, then you should see a solicitor or the Commission with a view to sending a form of questionnaire to the agent or vendor. For example:

iii   You are black. You see an advertisement for two adjoining houses on a small estate. You go to see the agent and are told that the houses have just been sold. The agent refuses any further explanation. The advertisement for the houses appears again the next week and the following week. You go to see the agent again and are told that when the properties were sold the agent forgot to cancel the advertising which had been arranged some weeks in advance. You do not believe this story. You see a solicitor and prepare the questionnaire to be sent to the agent. You say in the questionnaire that you believe that the agent has directly discriminated against you by refusing to sell either of the two houses to you. You also ask for the name and address of the purchaser of each of the two houses and the date when each purchaser first agreed to buy. You also ask for documentary evidence of this date, such as a copy of the receipt given for any holding deposit paid and a copy of the sale details sent to the vendor's and purchaser's solicitors. You point out that if copies of the documents are withheld and you bring proceedings the court will eventually order the production of the documents. The agent refuses to answer any of the questions. This refusal could go against the agent at the hearing of your complaint and it also encourages you to go ahead with proceedings.

Indirect discrimination

A person selling a house or flat cannot get away with discrimination by inventing some requirement or condition designed to eliminate most black or brown people. For example:

iv Your parents came from Pakistan. You telephone the vendor of a house in answer to a newspaper advertisement. When you tell him your name he says that he is not prepared to sell his house to a Muslim. There are two most likely possibilities. One is that this is not a genuine requirement at all and that if a West Indian Christian were to enquire about the house some other reason would be invented for not selling to him. In this event the discrimination against you has been direct, not indirect. The other most likely possibility is that the vendor has dreamed up his requirement deliberately to exclude potential buyers of Pakistani origin. In that event, even though the discrimination is indirect, the vendor will be ordered to pay damages if you win your case, since he will be unable to prove that the requirement was not racially motivated. You should commence proceedings claiming that there has been either direct discrimination or indirect discrimination against you.

Compensation

If you take proceedings for racial discrimination and win your case the judge will order the defendant to pay damages to you. The damages will include compensation for the injury to your feelings, although this will usually be a modest amount.

In addition, if you have incurred expenses in connection with your proposed purchase, you will be entitled to those expenses. If, for example, the vendor backs out just before the contracts stage, because of pressure from his neighbours, you will probably have paid a survey fee to a building society and also have a bill to pay to your solicitor. You can ask for damages to cover these expenses.

In addition, if you can show that the price at which the vendor was offering the house is less than the market value you may be able to claim the difference between the price and the market value. However, this could be very difficult to prove.

Offensive advertisements

If you walk past a house and see a sign in the garden or the window stating that the house is for sale to a white person only, you may feel very upset, even though you were not actually interested in buying the house. You cannot take any action yourself against the person displaying the offensive advertisement. However, if you report all the circumstances to the Commission for Racial Equality they will be able to consider taking action.

11

Applying for a loan for your purchase

If you apply for a loan to finance your purchase of a house or flat, the law does not permit any racial discrimination against you either in refusing the application or in imposing stiffer terms for the loan.

Private loans

Sometimes the vendor of a house or flat offers to leave part of the price owing to be paid by instalments under a private mortgage. This could happen if the property is in such bad condition that neither a building society nor a bank nor the local council would consider advancing money for the purchase of it.

If the vendor, on racial grounds, refuses to leave the money owing or puts up the rate of interest, this discrimination against you will be unlawful and you can take proceedings. For example:

i   You were one of the Asians expelled from East Africa and you came to Britain. You offer to buy a house which has been advertised for sale. The advertisement stated that a private mortgage would be available. The vendor is willing to sell you the house but tells you that you cannot have the mortgage because he does not want to run the risk that you will go back "home" before you have made all the payments. You point out that this is racial discrimination and ask him to reconsider. He then says that he will let you have the mortgage provided that you can find an "English" person to stand as a guarantor. This requirement that to obtain the mortgage you must have a guarantor is also direct discrimination, because it is not one which a white person would be asked to comply with. It would

126

also be direct discrimination if the vendor offered you the mortgage but at an extra two per cent interest to compensate him for the risk that you could leave the country without completing the payments.

Banks and building societies

Most loans for the purchase of houses and flats are obtained from banks, building societies, insurance companies and local authorities. If you face direct discrimination when you apply for a loan to any of these organisations it is likely to be unauthorised discrimination by a junior employee. For example:

ii   You are black. You go into a building society office to ask about an advance for the purchase of a house. You speak to a clerk who tells you that there are no funds available and that the society cannot consider your application at the moment. Her manner is very offhand and you suspect racial discrimination. You arrange for a white friend to go in and speak to the same clerk. He is told that the society will be prepared to consider an application for an advance and is given an application form. Unless some satisfactory explanation for the difference in treatment can be given, the clerk has directly discriminated against you. The society also has a legal liability, unless it can show that it has taken all reasonable steps to prevent this kind of discrimination. If you take proceedings, you should do so against both the society and against the clerk.

Before you actually take proceedings, and even before you use the questionnaire procedure to find out whether the society has a satisfactory explanation, there is one other thing which you should seriously consider doing. Presumably what you really want is not damages for discrimination but the mortgage advance for which you originally applied. You should therefore, either personally or preferably through your solicitor, approach the manager of the society, explain what has happened and ask if he will put the matter right. It is only if the manager refuses to discuss the matter or to accept your version of what has happened that you should consider going on to the next step, sending the formal questionnaire to the society. You must, however, bear in mind that no time must be lost in making an initial informal approach to the society or in sending the questionnaire, since if you are going to take proceedings you must do so within six months after the date of your initial conversation with the clerk at the society office.

The only kind of direct discrimination ever likely to be adopted by a local authority or large organisation as a deliberate policy is reverse or positive discrimination. For example, it would usually be direct discrimination if a local authority were to set aside a portion of its mortgage funds to be used exclusively for the benefit of applicants from ethnic minority groups. If you as a white person were to be refused a mortgage as a result of any such policy then you would obviously feel aggrieved. The council could however possibly have a defence to any proceedings on the ground that the special treatment of the ethnic minorities was designed to meet their special needs in regard to their welfare. For example:

iii   You are white and you apply to your local council for a mortgage. The town contains a large Bangladeshi community. Because there is a far greater problem of homelessness and inferior housing amongst this community than there is amongst the other people in the town the council has set aside a proportion of its funds in order to make advances to the Bangladeshis to enable them to improve their living conditions. Because of this quota and because all other funds have been used up your application for an advance is unsuccessful. On the face of it you have been a victim of direct racial discrimination, but the council would possibly have a successful defence on the ground that their action was designed to meet the special welfare needs of the Bangladeshis.

Indirect discrimination

If you are refused a loan because you cannot comply with some requirement which appears to be indirectly discriminatory, you should always bear one point in mind before you decide to take proceedings. If the building society or other organisation to which you apply for a loan can show the requirement to be justifiable, then you will lose your case.

For example:

iv   You are black. You apply to a building society for a mortgage. You are told that the society is short of funds and is lending money only to people who have been investing with the society for at least twelve months. The requirement, that to obtain a loan you must have been an investing member for this period, is one with which you cannot comply. You may also be able to show that the proportion of black people who might want a mortgage and cannot comply with the requirement is considerably greater than the corresponding proportion of white people. However, the society would not find it hard to defeat your claim by satisfying the judge that the requirement was justifiable. The societies need investors and it is good commercial practice for them to encourage people to invest by giving priority to investors when it comes to lending money.

12

Looking for rented accommodation

The general rule is that people and organisations who have accommodation to let must not discriminate against you by turning down your application for a tenancy, by charging you a higher rent or otherwise imposing stiffer terms on you or by refusing to put you on a waiting list. It does not matter whether the accommodation which you are seeking is a house or a flat or a single room. The discrimination against you is unlawful whether the person discriminating is the owner of the premises or an agent.

Is discrimination ever permitted?

The exception mentioned in Chapter 10 about disposals by owner-occupiers would also apply where premises are let by the owner if he has been occupying them. However, this exception is not important in practice, because it applies only when no agent has been employed and no advertising at all has been used.

The only important exception to the general rule is that racial discrimination is sometimes permitted when the tenants will be sharing some kind of living accommodation with the landlord or a near relative of his. The accommodation which is shared must be something more than the entrance hall and staircase or storage accommodation. For example, the accommodation to be shared could include a kitchen or a bathroom or a laundry room.

Even when there is shared accommodation, discrimination is only allowed if the premises are what the Act refers to as "small premises". The meaning of "small premises" can best be illustrated by two examples:

i   You apply for the tenancy of a self-contained flat and are turned
      down because of your colour. In the building there are two other
      similar flats, one of which is occupied by the owner of the
      building and his family. The tenants of all three flats share the
      use of a laundry room. The discrimination against you is lawful.
      If there had been a fourth flat, then the premises would not have
      qualified as "small premises" and the discrimination would have
      been unlawful.

ii   Your application for a room in a boarding house is turned down
      because of your colour. The house contains the living quarters of
      the owner and his family, rooms for six boarders and a dining
      room which is shared by the family and the boarders. The
      discrimination against you is lawful. If there had been rooms
      for seven boarders then the discrimination would have been
      unlawful because the premises would not have been "small
      premises".

Presumably the reason for the above exception is that if people are
racially prejudiced it can do no good to make them share their homes
with the people against whom they are prejudiced. The exception is
similar to that which permits racial discrimination in the employment
of persons for the purposes of a private household.

Direct discrimination by private landlords

Previous experience of tenants who are the same colour or ethnic
origin as you can never be a lawful excuse for racial discrimination
against you. For example:

iii   You are West Indian and you apply for the tenancy of a flat. The
      "small premises" exception does not apply, because the landlord
      does not live on the premises and nor does any near relative of
      his. The landlord tells you that he is not prepared to offer you a
      tenancy, because the previous tenants were West Indian and they
      caused trouble by holding noisy parties. This racial
      discrimination against you is unlawful. Penalising people for the
      real or supposed sins of others who happen to have the same
      colour or racial origin is one of the kinds of discrimination which
      the law is designed to stamp out.

The racial discrimination against you is equally unlawful if the landlord is not prejudiced against you but prejudiced in favour of people belonging to his own racial group. For example:

iv   You are of Asian origin. You apply for the tenancy of a house which is owned by a West Indian. He tells you that he has nothing at all against Asians, but he proposes to let his house only to a fellow West Indian. This racial discrimination against you is unlawful.

Sometimes the racial discrimination is of a less straightforward kind. For example:

v   You are white and your girl friend is black. You apply for the tenancy of a flat where you want to live together. The landlord turns you down. He has both white tenants and black tenants but he is not prepared to have a white person and a black person living together in one of his flats. This racial discrimination against you is unlawful. It would be different if the landlord objected only because you are unmarried and if he were willing to take you as tenants if you get married first.

Recognising and proving discrimination

It is not often that landlords will openly admit that they are turning down your application for accommodation on racial grounds. The most common excuse given is that the property which you are after has already been let. Even if you suspect, from the landlord's evasive manner, that this is a false reason, how can you prove discrimination? The most common way is to arrange for a white friend to enquire about the same property. If the friend is told that the property is still available and is offered a chance to view the property then you have some evidence of discrimination. It is very important that both you and your white friend should make a very full and careful note of your conversations with the landlord. For example:

vi   You are black. You ring up about a flat which you have seen advertised. The landlord tells you that the flat has already been taken. You then arrange for a white friend to ring up about the same flat and the landlord offers him an appointment to view the flat. You subsequently bring proceedings against the landlord.

The landlord denies that he told you that the flat had been taken. He said that he got the impression, from something you said to him on the telephone, that you had a large family and that he told you that the flat would be too small for you. Unless you have kept a full note of exactly what you and the landlord said to each other on the telephone you may find it difficult to disprove this statement.

Once you are sure that racial discrimination has occurred, because you and your white friend have been given different answers by the landlord, you should then immediately consult the Commission for Racial Equality or a solicitor or a law centre and arrange to send the landlord the formal questionnaire which is available under the Race Relations Act. In the questionnaire, you will give the address of the property which you applied for and the date on which the landlord turned down your application for a tenancy and state that you believe that this was an act of racial discrimination against you. You will ask the landlord on what grounds he states that your application was refused. You will also ask him for the name and address of any person to whom the property has now been let and the date of that letting.

If the landlord has told you that you cannot have the flat because it has already been let but he has in fact let the property to somebody else a week or two after the conversation with you, then the landlord will be in some difficulty in completing the form. It would be dangerous for the landlord simply to give a false date for the letting, because if you take proceedings you will be able to insist on the production of relevant documents, such as the rent book and a copy of any receipt given for the first payment of rent, and you could also if necessary ask for a witness summons requiring the tenant to come along and give evidence (although it can be risky to enforce the attendance of a witness who could be hostile).

Accommodation agencies

Many people who have a house or flat to let place the property on the books of an agent. You may go along to an agency either because they are dealing with some particular property which you are interested in or because you know that they have properties on their books in the area where you would like to live. What should you do if you are told, in an evasive sort of way, that the property which you are after has already been let or that there are no suitable properties in the area where you want to live? You should do much the same as you would do if you suspected discrimination by a landlord with whom you were dealing. For example:

vii   You are coloured. You have heard that an accommodation agency has a number of properties to let in the area where you wish to live and you go along to their offices. You are given details of only two properties, neither of which is suitable. You then arrange for a white friend to go along to ask about properties in the same area and this friend is given details of ten properties. You then go back a second time and again are told that the only properties are the two which have been previously shown to you. You use the questionnaire procedure, which brings no satisfactory explanation from the agency, and you commence proceedings. Before the proceedings you obtain, through your solicitor, an order for the production of the agency's records relating both to the two properties which you were shown and the other eight which were mentioned to your white friend. The cards for these eight properties have coded symbols which do not appear on the cards for the two properties which you saw. In the absence of any explanation from the agency the judge concludes that the special markings on the eight cards indicate that the agency has received instructions to offer those properties only to white tenants. Your claim against the agency succeeds.

Whenever you take proceedings against an agency you should consider also suing the owner of the premises, if you know his or her name and address. The owner is liable as well as the agent unless the discrimination was unauthorised.

Even if you decide not to take proceedings against an agency which you suspect of discriminating against you, you should report the facts to the Commission for Racial Equality. The Commission has the power to carry out a formal investigation and is likely to use that power where it receives a number of complaints in respect of an agency and suspects widespread discrimination by the agency.

Local authority accommodation

Local authorities are one of the country's major sources of housing accommodation. At one time some authorities used to discriminate in favour of applicants who had British nationality. Until the current Race Relations Act came into force that kind of discrimination was lawful. It is now unlawful for a council to refuse to consider a person's application for a tenancy on the ground that that person is not a British citizen.

If a council were to insist on a residential requirement before placing you on the waiting list for a council property this requirement could possibly amount to indirect discrimination against you. For example:

viii You came to England from Pakistan six months ago and since then you have been living in inferior accommodation in a town. You are not eligible for a place on the waiting list for council accommodation until you have lived in the country for a year. The council would find it very difficult to justify its requirement. If on the other hand the council had a requirement that all applicants (other than the homeless seeking emergency accommodation), however long they had lived in England, must have lived in the town itself for at least twelve months in order to be eligible for council accommodation, a court would be much more likely to find this requirement to be justifiable. Moreover you can have no complaint if the council does not have a strict residential requirement but simply uses the length of your residence either in the country or in the town itself as one of several factors to be taken into account in determining your place on the waiting list.

13

Your rights as a tenant

If you are the tenant of a privately rented house or flat you will have important rights under the Rent Acts. Even if there were no Race Relations Act, you would be able to take proceedings against your landlord if he harassed you or refused to carry out repairs for which he is responsible or unlawfully evicted you. If you have occasion to take any such proceedings and if you feel that your landlord singled you out on racial grounds for harsh treatment it will often be sensible for you to add a claim under the Race Relations Act to your other claims against the landlord. If that claim is upheld, the court will be able to award you damages to compensate you for the injury to your feelings, in addition to any damages awarded to you in respect of your claim under the Rent Acts.

Discrimination by landlord's employees

What if you have no complaint against your landlord personally but one of the landlord's employees, such as a rent collector, behaves in an aggressive and abusive way towards you. If the rent collector behaves in this way because of your colour or on some other racial ground, you could have a claim under the Race Relations Act both against the rent collector and against your landlord. The landlord, whether a private landlord or a local authority, would have a defence to the claim only if it could be shown that all reasonably practicable steps had been taken to prevent the kind of discrimination complained of.

Transfers of council houses

Private tenants have for years now had the protection of the Rent Acts. Tenants of council houses also now have certain rights, under the Housing Act 1980. However, complaints of racial discrimination are probably in practice more likely to arise not because of any alleged breach of those rights but because of the council's attitude towards applications for a transfer from one house or estate to another. For example:

i   You are a black tenant of a house on a council estate and you are being harassed by your white neighbours. You complain to the council. You are told that the council will transfer your neighbours to another estate only if you accept a transfer as well. The council feel that where a dispute has broken out between a white family and a black family it could cause racial tension if only the white family were to be transferred. You protest, pointing out that you are the innocent party, but the council refuse to change the decision. By treating you less favourably than they would have treated a white tenant who complained about a white neighbour the council have directly and unlawfully discriminated against you.

In the above example, the discrimination would be equally unlawful if you were a white tenant complaining about persecution by your black neighbours and the council, afraid of causing racial tension, refused to move your black neighbours unless you agreed to move as well. It would also be unlawful if a council were to adopt a policy of racial segregation, however benevolent the motive. For example:

ii   You are of Asian origin. You live on a council estate on which all your neighbours are also Asians. You apply for a transfer to another estate because you wish your children to have the opportunity of mixing with children of all colours and improving their command of English. The council refuse to consider your request, because they have a policy of putting all the Asian families together for mutual help and support. It is pointed out to you that the houses on the estate where you are now are of better quality than the houses on the estate to which you wish to be transferred. The direct discrimination against you is unlawful.

137

The Race Relations Act forbids racial segregation and it is no defence to show that the facilities afforded to you are equal to those which you would have received even if there had been no segregation.

You could also have a successful claim against a council which adopted an opposite policy. For example:

iii   You are of West Indian origin and you live on an estate where all your neighbours are white. You apply for a transfer to another estate, where two of your West Indian friends live. The council refuses to consider the request, because the council has a policy of dispersing ethnic minorities throughout its council estates, on the theory that if people of different colours and races have to live together they are more likely to learn mutual understanding and respect. This direct discrimination against you is unlawful.

The only lawful approach for a council to adopt is to treat every application for a transfer on its merits and not to be influenced in any way by the colour of the person making the request or by any other racial factor.

If, as a council tenant, you feel that you have been the victim of racial discrimination, perhaps on the part of a junior official in the housing department, you should consider making an approach to the council at a higher level before commencing proceedings. You should not delay seeing the Commission for Racial Equality or a solicitor or a law centre about your complaint, because you have only six months in which to commence proceedings and you will want to submit your application for legal aid or application to the Commission for assistance as quickly as possible. However, whilst you are waiting for the result of your application for legal aid or your application to the Commission you could profitably use the intervening time by making an informal approach to a more senior officer of the council or to your local councillor. If you can obtain redress without having to go to court this will save you a good deal of time and trouble.

Part IV
Other acts of discrimination

In this Part we shall look at your rights as a student and your rights in connection with the education of your children. Before these, there are the rights which the Act gives you as a member of the public. There must be no racial discrimination against you by any person concerned with the provision of goods, facilities or services to the public or a section of the public. They must not discriminate by refusing to supply or serve you or in the way in which they supply or serve you.

Even government departments, when they are supplying some kind of facility or service, must not discriminate, except where the discrimination is authorised by statute. There was a successful claim recently against the Inland Revenue by a taxpayer born in India. He had been required to produce a full birth certificate in order to claim an allowance for a dependent child, although short forms of birth certificates were accepted from other taxpayers. This racial discrimination against taxpayers born overseas was held to be unlawful.

In this Part, the claims which you are most likely to have in practice as a member of the public are dealt with in two separate chapters. First of all, there are claims which you may have as a consumer, wishing to buy or hire goods or services, including insurance. Then there are your rights as a person seeking access to places of entertainment and recreation including pubs, dance halls, nightclubs, hotels and restaurants. In this chapter we shall look not only at your rights as a member of the public but also at your rights when you wish to join or go into a private club.

If you have a claim about any of the matters discussed in this Part of the book you must commence proceedings in the county court within six months after the discrimination which you are complaining about. You may apply for legal aid. You should read Chapter 9 of the book, because the information and advice contained in that chapter is relevant to this Part of the book as well as to Part III.

14

Your rights as a consumer

You have the right not to meet racial discrimination whenever you go into a shop or supermarket to buy goods. You have this right also when you wish to buy a service, for instance from a dentist or a plumber or a hairdresser. You also have the right when you wish to take advantage of some facility provided to the public or a section of the public, such as transport on a bus, coach or train.

Goods and services

You only have a claim when the goods, facilities or services which you are after are to be provided in Great Britain or on a British ship or aircraft. However, there must be no discrimination in Great Britain by a travel agent or tour operator even when they are offering overseas holidays. For example:

i   You are black. You apply to a tour operator for a place on a package holiday to Spain. The literature produced by the tour operator states that rooms in the hotel in Spain will be shared. You are offered the last place on the holiday but this offer is then withdrawn when the company find out about your colour. The place offered to you involves sharing a room with a white person who has expressly stipulated that he will share only with another white person. The racial discrimination against you by the tour operator is unlawful.

Most people selling goods or services to the public are not so well off that they can afford to turn away customers to satisfy any racial prejudice that they may have. However, prejudice could come to the surface and result in discrimination when you go back to a shop with a complaint. For example:

ii   You are of Asian origin. You buy goods from a shop and take them back because they are faulty. The shopkeeper refuses to listen to your complaint and is abusive towards you. Unless the shopkeeper can show that he behaves in the same abusive way to all customers who have complaints, whatever their colour, he is discriminating against you unlawfully by refusing you the service, that of dealing courteously with complaints, which would be offered to a white customer.

What if a doctor or dentist or accountant or some other professional person refuses to see you because you cannot speak English? Is this indirect discrimination? A court would probably hold it to be unjustifiable for a professional man to refuse outright to see a patient or client who could not speak English. However, it would almost certainly be held justifiable for a professional man to insist that you take with you a friend able to speak English well and to translate for you since inability to communicate properly could result in the wrong advice or treatment being given to you.

Credit and finance

There must be no discrimination against you in the provision of credit or finance, for instance by a bank or finance company. Sometimes stores offer their own credit terms and they must not discriminate either. For example:

iii   You are an American citizen living in Great Britain. You apply to a finance company for a loan to buy a car. You are told by the company that because you are a foreign national you may have a loan only if a British citizen signs the loan agreement to guarantee the repayments. This direct discrimination against you on the ground of your nationality is unlawful.

Discrimination against you not because of your nationality but because of where you live could amount to indirect discrimination. For example:

iv   You are black and about half the people in the district where you live are black also. You go into a store to buy some furniture. The store has offered to supply the furniture on easy terms, but when they find out where you live they tell you that to have the furniture you must pay the full price in advance. The reason is that previous customers, both black and white, from your district have defaulted in their payments. The requirement that in order to have credit you should not live in the district where you do live is indirectly discriminatory against you and is one which almost certainly would not be held to be justifiable. However, if you took proceedings against the company you would not be entitled to damages if the company could show that the requirement was in no way racially motivated.

Insurance

There must be no racial discrimination by insurance companies, either when deciding whether to issue a policy to you or in fixing the premium rates. For instance if you have a driving licence you must not be refused insurance simply because you are a foreign national. Racial grounds must play no part at all in the way in which the insurance company deals with you, even where there would be an actuarial basis for treating you differently. For example:

v   You are of overseas origin and you apply for life insurance. The statistics show that men and women born in your country have a slightly lower life expectancy than people born in Great Britain. Consequently the insurance company fix a slightly higher premium. This direct discrimination against you is unlawful.

The above example is hypothetical. The kind of discrimination more likely in practice is indirect discrimination. For example:

vi   You have come to Great Britain from India where you drove a car for many years. You buy a car in Great Britain and apply for insurance. The insurance company tell you that they require all drivers, of whatever origin, to pay a higher premium during their first twelve months of driving in Great Britain, since until people have experience of British road conditions they have a higher risk of accidents. The requirement that to pay a lower premium you must have twelve months experience of driving in Britain is indirectly discriminatory against you, because a person born in Britain, who has the same amount of driving experience as you but has had that experience in Great Britain, would be able to comply with the requirement, whilst you cannot. The requirement would possibly be held to be justifiable. It would certainly not be justifiable if you had to pay the higher premium for a much longer period than could be necessary to gain experience of British driving conditions. If for example you had to pay the higher premium for ten years then the indirect discrimination against you would be unlawful.

It is lawful for an insurance company to refuse to insure overseas property or to charge a higher premium.

15

Entertainment and recreation

There must be no racial discrimination against you when you try to enter a hotel, restaurant, pub, nightclub, dance hall, cinema or any other place of public entertainment or recreation. There must be no discrimination either in refusing you service or in refusing to treat you like other customers.

Direct discrimination

The following example is based on an actual case:

i   You are of Indian origin and you go into a public house. The landlord refuses to serve you in the lounge bar and tells you that he will serve you in the tap room. You are wearing a suit and are more smartly dressed than several white customers who are in the lounge bar. You are also quiet and sober and well behaved. If you have been required to use the tap room rather than the lounge bar because of your colour, then this is direct racial discrimination against you and you have a claim against the landlord.

It is now uncommon for the management of any place of entertainment or recreation to refuse entry to you and to be quite open about saying that this is because of your colour. When open discrimination of this kind does happen it is usually because a collective ban has been imposed following previous disturbances. The following example is also based on an actual case:

ii   You were born in the West Indies. You are refused admission to a dance hall. There is nothing at all against you personally. A temporary ban was imposed on all West Indians following a disturbance some months earlier. The direct racial discrimination against you is unlawful. People must be judged on their merits as individuals and not made to suffer for the faults of others who simply happen to have the same colour.

The result in the above example would have been different if you had been personally associated with trouble makers. For example:

iii You are of Asian origin. You are in a public house with a group of friends and one of your friends starts a fight. You go back to the pub the following evening and the landlord refuses to serve you. He tells you that you and all your friends are banned because of the fight that was started the previous night. If you were to take proceedings against the landlord he would be successful in defending your claim provided that he could satisfy the court that he would have banned every member of a party of white youths in similar circumstances.

Usually, if the management of a dance hall or nightclub wish to keep you out because of your colour, some different reason will be given to you. The following example is also based on an actual case:

iv You are of African origin. You and a friend, also of African origin, go to a nightclub and are refused entry. You are both smartly dressed and you have not been drinking. You are told that you cannot go in because you are not members. In order to become members you would have to be proposed by a member. You arrange for two white friends to go to the nightclub the following evening. Your friends are allowed in without question, even though they are not members. They are less smartly dressed than you are. You then go along five minutes later and ask again to be allowed in. You are again refused entry because you are not members. It is likely that your claim against the club would succeed, because the club would find it very difficult to give a satisfactory explanation for the different treatment of you and your white friends.

Often the person who actually discriminates against you will be an employee of the owner of the premises. For instance if you are turned away from a nightclub it would usually be the doorman who speaks to you. When racial discrimination occurs you may take proceedings both against the employee who actually discriminates against you and against his or her employer. The latter will have a defence only if it can be proved that all reasonably practicable steps have been taken to prevent the kind of discrimination which you are complaining of.

There is no racial discrimination when you are turned away from premises for a reason which genuinely has nothing to do with your colour or any other racial ground, even though the person turning you away is mistaken. For example:

v   You are black. You wish to enter a nightclub. Because of an illness you are unsteady on your feet. The doorman genuinely believes that you are drunk and refuses to allow you in for that reason. Any white person who appeared to be drunk would also not be allowed in. There has been no racial discrimination against you, even though the doorman was mistaken in believing you were drunk.

Indirect discrimination

If you are refused entry or service because you cannot speak English or because you are wearing a turban or a sari, the question of indirect racial discrimination will arise only if this is a genuine reason. If the real reason for not allowing you in or not serving you is your colour, then the discrimination is direct. When the requirement is genuine, then the question of indirect discrimination arises. There would possibly be no unlawful discrimination in the following example:

vi   You are of Asian origin and you are refused entry to a public house because you cannot speak English. The pub is a very small one and the landlord likes to create a friendly atmosphere by engaging all the customers in conversation. He has a number of Asian customers who can speak English fluently. It is possible (although by no means certain) that a court would hold his language requirement to be justifiable.

A language requirement could also be upheld if you were seeking entry into any kind of establishment where it is essential that you should be able to understand what is going on, such as a bingo hall. On the other hand, for example:

vii You are of Asian origin and you are refused entry to a public house because you cannot speak English. This is a large

147

establishment with several large bars in which customers sit at small tables. There is no general conversation. The indirect discrimination against you would almost certainly be held to be unlawful.

It is also unlikely that any establishment open to the public could get away with banning you because as a Sikh, you wear a turban.

Private clubs

If you wish to play sport, you may take advantage of facilities made available by the local council. There must be no racial discrimination in the provision of those facilities.

You may, however, wish to join a private sports club. You may also wish to join a private social club. Under the current Race Relations Act, there must be no racial discrimination by a club in the way in which it deals with applications for membership, in the way in which it treats its members or in the way in which it treats members of affiliated clubs.

It may be easy for you to recognise and prove discrimination if you are refused entry to a club of which you have some kind of associate membership. For example:

viii You belong to a club which is part of a national association of clubs and the rules give you associate membership of clubs in other towns which belong to the association. You are black. You and a white friend try to enter a club in another town which belongs to the association. Your white friend is allowed in but you are refused entry. Unless some satisfactory explanation can be given for the difference in treatment then you have a claim against the club for direct racial discrimination.

It may be more difficult to prove racial discrimination by a club dealing with your application for membership, because clubs do not usually give a reason for refusing applications for membership. However, the questionnaire procedure under the Race Relations Act will enable you to ask for the reason before you take proceedings against the club. For example:

ix You are black. You apply for membership of a private sports club. Your application is refused. No reason for the refusal is

148

given. You use the questionnaire procedure, stating that you believe that the club may have refused you membership on racial grounds and you ask for the reasons why your application was turned down. You are told that your application has been refused because you have only lived in the area for a couple of years. However, you find out through your proposer that a white applicant has been offered membership even though he has lived in the area for only six months. You can therefore commence proceedings with some confidence that they will be successful. It may be difficult for you to show that the refusal of your application has caused you any financial loss, but you are entitled to damages for the injury to your feelings.

Exceptions

There are two exceptions to the law relating to private clubs. First of all, clubs and associations with fewer than twenty five members are exempt. Secondly, a club or association may lawfully have as its main object the provision of the benefits of membership to "persons of a particular racial group defined otherwise than by reference to colour". It is, for instance, lawful to establish clubs or associations for the exclusive benefit of West Indians living in Great Britain or South Africans living in Great Britain. However, it would not be lawful for a club for West Indians to refuse to have white West Indians as members or for a club for South Africans to refuse to have black or coloured South Africans as members.

16

Education

The Race Relations Act applies to educational establishments in the public sector, such as primary schools, secondary schools and technical colleges maintained by local education authorities and to most polytechnics. It also applies to establishments in the private sector, such as independent schools and universities.

Racial discrimination is forbidden against you personally, if you are a student or want to be one, and against your child. There must be no discrimination in dealing with applications for admission to an educational establishment. Claims can also arise if there is discrimination against pupils or students who are at an educational establishment.

Admission to schools

If any local education authority were to adopt a policy of "busing" children on racial grounds, you could bring a claim against the authority if your child suffered as a result. For example:

i   You want your child, who is white, to go to the neighbourhood school. However, the local education authority insist that your child must travel to a school several miles away, not because the school is more suitable for your child, but as part of the "busing" policy. The authority are "busing" white children away from white areas and black children away from black areas in order to enable children to mix with children from different ethnic backgrounds. Your child is being made to travel long distances on racial grounds and this racial discrimination is unlawful, however well meaning the motive. It would be different if a

150

council selected children on non-racial grounds for schools outside their own areas.

If your child is refused a place at a school because he or she is of the wrong religion, this is not direct racial discrimination, but is it indirect discrimination? For example:

ii You are of Pakistani origin. Your son, like you, is a Muslim. He is refused a place at a school which is for Anglicans only. The requirement that to qualify for a place at the school a child must be Anglican appears to be indirectly discriminatory against your child and other Pakistanis, most of whom are Muslims. However the requirement would probably be held to be justifiable, since it is a legitimate object of a school to seek to promote a particular religion. The school must, of course, select genuinely on religious grounds and make places available for black, brown and yellow Anglicans.

It could also be lawful if a school set up only for Muslim children were to refuse entry to non-Muslims, even though on the face of it the entry requirement would be indirectly discriminatory against white children.

Charitable foundations and awards

If the school in the above example is an independent charitable foundation, the court will probably not even need to consider whether the entry requirement is justifiable. If a school or college has been endowed by a charitable trust, racial discrimination, except direct discrimination on the ground of colour, is lawful when the discrimination is necessary in order to give effect to the terms of the trust. Even if the trust requires that there be direct discrimination in the admission of children, this is lawful provided that it is not on grounds of colour. For example:

iii You are living in Scotland but you and your children were born in England. Your child is turned down for a place at an independent school because the school was endowed by a charitable foundation solely for the purpose of educating children born in Scotland. The direct racial discrimination against you is lawful. However the school could not lawfully discriminate against black children born in Scotland, whatever the terms of the trust.

There may also be discrimination in the award of prizes and scholarships when this is necessary to comply with the terms of a charitable trust. For example:

iv You and your elder son were born in India. Your younger son was born in Lancashire. They both go to an independent school at which pupils can compete for a university scholarship. Under the terms of the charitable trust only boys born in Lancashire are eligible for the scholarship. Your elder son can lawfully be refused a chance of competing for the scholarship but your younger son cannot, even if the trust specifies that candidates must be white. The latter requirement must be disregarded by the trustees.

Indirect discrimination

The question of indirect discrimination could arise if your child's religion or the custom of your community prevents your child from complying with a school's requirement about school uniform. You may face this problem when the child is applying for a place at a school and you are asked for an assurance that the child will wear school uniform or you may not have to face the problem until the child actually starts attending the school. For example:

v Your daughter, who like you is a Muslim of Pakistani origin, is awarded a place at a comprehensive school. Your daughter goes along to the school on her first day wearing trousers, for religious reasons. Your daughter is told that she must come to school in a dress in future. Is this requirement unlawful? There is little doubt that you and your daughter will succeed in a claim of indirect discrimination. A requirement that girls must not wear trousers affects a considerably greater proportion of girls of Pakistani origin than of other girls. The requirement is one with which your daughter and other Pakistani children *cannot* comply. In the recent case mentioned on Page 6 in the Introduction a stricter definition of "cannot comply" was rejected by the House of Lords. It is also clear from this case that the school authorities will have great difficulty if they try to show the requirement to be justifiable.

In the above mentioned case, Lord Fraser gave an example of a requirement which could in certain circumstances be held to be justifiable. He said "it might be possible for the school to show that a rule insisting upon a fixed diet, which included some dish (for example, pork) which some racial groups could not conscientiously eat was justifiable if the school proved that the cost of providing special meals for the particular group would be prohibitive".

Discrimination at school

Discrimination at school is lawful if it is designed to meet the special needs of members of an ethnic minority. For example:

vi You are white. Your son attends a school where there are many black and brown children, a number of whom cannot read or write English. These children are given special language classes. You ask for your child to be included in these classes because he is very backward at reading and writing. Your request is refused. You have no claim, because the Act permits special treatment of ethnic minorities in order to meet their special needs in regard to education.

Unless covered by the above exception, segregation on racial grounds is always unlawful. For example:

vii You were born in the West Indies, but your daughter was born in England. She attends a comprehensive school at which the white and the black children are put in different classes for certain lessons. For example whilst the white children are reading Shakespeare the black children are reading the works of lesser known black writers in order to give them a sense of black culture. You object to this segregation because you want your child to be prepared for life in England and not to be made to look backwards towards a West Indian culture which is now irrelevant to the child's needs or backwards to a still more remote African heritage. If an informal approach to the school or education authorities is unsuccessful then you should take legal advice on your prospects of a claim of direct discrimination.

Direct discrimination in disciplinary matters is also unlawful. For example:

viii Your child, who is white, and a black child are caught bullying. They both have equally bad records but the black child is let off with a warning whilst your child is expelled. Unless some satisfactory explanation can be given for the different treatment of the two children your child appears to have been treated unfavourably on racial grounds and this discrimination is unlawful.

A decision about some punishment less extreme than expulsion could be made by an individual teacher without the express authority of the education authorities or the managers or governors. If your child is singled out by a teacher on racial grounds, you may bring proceedings against both the teacher and his or her employers. The employers will be able to escape responsibility only if they have taken all reasonably practicable steps to prevent the kind of discrimination which you are complaining of.

Further education

The question of positive discrimination in admitting students is most likely to arise in connection with establishments of further education, especially universities. Is it lawful for a university to relax its entry requirements for members of an ethnic minority group? For example:

ix You are white. You apply for a place at a university, which requires applicants to have three 'A' levels. The university has resolved to relax this requirement for applicants belonging to certain ethnic minority groups. The reason is that many children in these groups have had to overcome serious educational difficulties, such as having to learn a new language or having their education disrupted by a move from one country to another. You are refused a place on a course because you have only two 'A' levels, but some black and brown students are allowed in with only one 'A' level. You would probably succeed in an action for racial discrimination against the governing body of the university. It is very doubtful whether the "special needs" exception would apply, because the ethnic minority youngsters

154

do not have a special need of university education any more than you do. What they need, or have needed, is extra coaching at school in order to overcome their language and other difficulties and to put them on an equal footing with you when competing for a university place.

Overseas students

There is one respect in which the Race Relations Act does permit direct discrimination in deciding who should be admitted to an educational establishment. Special provision may be made for students who are not ordinarily resident in Great Britain and who intend to leave Great Britain after their period of education or training here.

There is no corresponding discrimination in favour of overseas students when local authorities are handing out grants for further education. On the contrary, overseas students who apply for a grant are usually refused one if they have not been ordinarily resident in the United Kingdom for at least three years immediately prior to the start of the course. This discrimination against them is lawful because it is expressly authorised by statute.

It has recently been held by the courts* that a student is ordinarily resident in Great Britain even when he or she has no intention of living permanently in the country and is here only for educational purposes.

However the Government has acted to reverse the effects of this decision as from 31st March 1983.

Procedure

If your claim is about discrimination by a university or independent school, then proceedings should be started in the county court and there is no difference between your claim and any other claim which is outside the employment field. If, however, you wish to complain about discrimination in the public sector, you must give notice of your claim to the Secretary of State Education before commencing proceedings.

* Shah v. Barnet London Borough Council [1983] 1 All England Reports 226.

When you have given notice, you must then wait for two months before commencing proceedings, unless the Secretary of State notifies you within that period that no further time for consideration of the matter is required. Because of this special provision, the period of six months within which you must commence proceedings is extended to eight months. If you also apply to the Commission for Racial Equality for assistance there is a further extension of two months, making a total period of ten months.

Part V

The self-employed

If you have your own business, you are more likely to be on the receiving end of claims than making claims against other people. If you discriminate against your employees they can take you to an industrial tribunal and if you discriminate against customers they can take proceedings against you in the county court. If on the other hand an employee walks out on racial grounds or customers refuse to patronise you because they do not like the colour of your skin then there is nothing that you can do about it.

However, you do have a few rights as a self employed person and some of these are considered in Chapter 17. If you wish to complain about discrimination by a trade or employers' organisation or a qualifying body then you must take your case to an industrial tribunal and you should read Chapter 5. Other claims must be made to a county court and you should read Chapter 9.

17

Starting or running a business

Looking for premises

There must be no direct or indirect racial discrimination against you when you are trying to buy or rent premises for your business. For example:

i You are of Indian origin. You apply for the tenancy of a shop. The landlord tells you that the previous tenant was an Indian and defaulted in payment of the rent. Accordingly you can have the tenancy only if you can find a white person to guarantee that you will pay the rent. This direct racial discrimination against you is unlawful. Before you actually commence proceedings you should use the questionnaire procedure to ask the landlord on what grounds he required you to provide a guarantor and whether he has required any previous tenant or applicant for a tenancy to find a guarantor.

What if there is no direct racial discrimination but the landlord imposes requirements which you cannot comply with? For example:

ii You are of West Indian origin. You apply for the tenancy of a workshop in order to start your own business there. The landlord says that he will grant you a tenancy on production of satisfactory bank and trade references. The landlord assures you, and you believe him, that it is a standard practice to require references, whether the prospective tenant is white or black. You cannot produce any references, because you have never been in business before. You feel that the landlord's requirement is indirectly discriminatory against you as a West Indian, because the proportion of West Indians who have no business experience and cannot comply with the requirement is considerably greater than the proportion of people who are not West Indians. However, the landlord would probably be able to show the requirement to be justifiable, since it is legitimate on commercial grounds that a landlord should be able to satisfy himself that a tenant will be able to pay the rent.

If you are acquiring business premises not direct from the landlord but from a previous tenant, the landlord's licence or consent will usually be required. In that event, the landlord is under the same obligation not to discriminate against you by refusing or withholding consent as he would be if he was considering whether to grant a tenancy to you.

Looking for finance

If you wish to raise money for your business, you may apply to a bank or finance company for a loan or to a public body of some kind for a grant. There must be no direct or indirect racial discrimination against you by any of these bodies. However, a loan may lawfully be refused for a business venture outside Great Britain. For example:

iii   You are French and you approach a bank in England for a loan to enable you to open a factory in England and another one in France. The bank must not turn down the loan for the English factory simply because you are French. This would be direct racial discrimination. However, the bank can lawfully refuse to consider granting you a loan to open the French factory, even though on the face of it this refusal is indirectly discriminatory against you as a Frenchman.

The question of indirect discrimination could arise when a bank asks an overseas resident for collateral security. For example:

iv   You are a business man from the Middle East. You apply to a bank in England for a loan to start a new business in Great Britain. The bank asks you to put up your house or some other property in this country as collateral security, but you are unable to do so because you live in the Middle East and all your property is there. The requirement that collateral security should be provided is apparently indirectly discriminatory against you as a

160

foreign national, but it is one which the bank would probably have no difficulty in justifying as being a necessary commercial precaution.

Trade suppliers

Manufacturers and wholesalers must not discriminate against you by refusing to supply you or in the terms on which they offer to supply you. For example:

v   You are an American citizen running a business in England. A trade supplier who usually gives customers thirty days credit requires you to pay for goods in advance. The reason given is that you are American and if you went home to America without paying for the goods the supplier may be unable to trace you. This direct racial discrimination against you is unlawful.

Trade organisations

You may wish to join a trade or employers' organisation. There must be no discrimination against you by refusing you membership or in the terms of membership. For example:

vi   You are a West German citizen with a business in England. You join a trade organisation which has one subscription rate for British subjects and a higher rate for foreign nationals. This direct discrimination against you is unlawful.

Qualifying bodies

Sometimes, in a trade or profession, it is helpful or even essential for you to have some sort of licence or qualification from some official or professional body. For instance if you wish to sell goods and offer credit to your customers you will need a licence under the Consumer Credit Act from the Director of Fair Trading. There must be no racial discrimination by any qualifying body, either by refusing to grant a licence or qualification to you or in the terms on which the licence or qualification is granted. For example:

vii   You were born in India and obtained a degree there. You have settled in Great Britain and wish to practise a profession. In order to obtain recognition from the governing body of the profession you must pass an examination. Graduates of British universities are exempt from the examination but the professional body refuses to allow you exemption on the strength of your Indian degree, even though it is equivalent in status to a degree from a British university. The requirement that to qualify for the exemption you must have a British degree is unlawful. The proportion of men and women of Indian origin who cannot comply with the requirement is greater than the proportion of those not of Indian origin and there are no grounds on which the requirement can be justified.

Appendix

Offices of the Commission for Racial Equality

HEADQUARTERS
Elliot House
10/12 Allington Street
London
SW1E 5EH
Tel: 01 828 7022

BIRMINGHAM
Stanier House
Fourth Floor
10 Holliday Street
Birmingham
B1 1TG
Tel: 021 632 4544

MANCHESTER
Maybrook House
40 Blackfriars Street
Manchester
M3 2EG
Tel: 061 831 7782/8

LEICESTER
Haymarket House
(4th Floor)
Haymarket Shopping Centre
Leicester
LE1 3YG
Tel: 0533 57852

LEEDS
133 The Headrow
Leeds
LS1 5QX
Tel: 0532 34413/4

Index